ANGRY MAN!
GO AWAY!

Angry Man!
Go Away!

Raje E. Voega

iUniverse, Inc.
Bloomington

ANGRY MAN! GO AWAY!

iUniverse books may be ordered through booksellers or by contacting:

iUniverse
1663 Liberty Drive
Bloomington, IN 47403
www.iuniverse.com
1-800-Authors (1-800-288-4677)

ISBN: 978-1-4759-8612-9 (sc)
ISBN: 978-1-4759-8614-3 (hc)
ISBN: 978-1-4759-8613-6 (ebk)

Printed in the United States of America

iUniverse rev. date: 04/16/2013

Dedicated to "B.M.M."

INTRODUCTION

I do not know where to start, so I will start with what brought me to this point. I just came out of a very rough relationship, it started well, however, there was an addiction, third girl in a row. I saw it from the beginning, I remember thinking every time she went to the VLT's that I should be crazy to go down that path again, however, I thought she was different. I was wrong, my fault. Her addiction went from the VLT's, to the computer, social networking sites and games.

After five years, four on again, off again, and having given her everything in my heart and mind she left me over the dumbest thing, her pride. I have been driven to a point that she said would never happen. She moved on instantly and I almost hurt her new boyfriend. I would have crossed that line, and it was close . . . being run off the road in a 100 km/h spin out would of flipped his truck I am sure. Then getting out of the car and finishing it . . . I am in a dark place right now, I guess the reason why I have been betrayed by most of my girlfriends was to get me to this point, to take this kind of hurt without taking the knowledge I have learnt in explosives, bomb making, weaponry, wiring, stalking, human hunting, forensics, psychology and using it. And with my ability to see the big picture, I have new ways to do things, build things, or eliminate things.

I have learnt how to drive and anticipate what others will do. I have followed countless people over the years, in some cases almost to the point of stalking them. I have learnt how to stay in the shadows, to hide in plain site without being seen, in a car or on foot. To see something coming and try to counter it or out think it, takes practice and patience.

Love blinds you, signs that were in front of you, signs that you were stumbling over and some that hit you hard in the face, are all ignored because the thought of being alone forever is everyone's fear, and those few who don't fear it, I envy. When you find love, someone says they love you, then leave you, it is amazing how much it takes to stay in control, this is one of those stories. How to stay in control, even if you're not sure how.

At the time of writing this book, I am thirty-six years old, living in Southern Alberta, and I have no biological children. I say that with a little hesitation, although I am not her biological parent, you will read about an ex-girlfriend who is named Subject X, who has this little girl that is just amazing. She is seven years old with blond hair and a smile that could melt the sun. I loved Subject X and fell in love with a family that wasn't mine, and never was going to be mine.

In the end I was thrown away, but it is my own fault. I saw the signs over the years, but I was to close to stay away. They say you can't change a person, they say do not expect that person to change. What happens if that person says they want to change, what if they say they want all same things you want? And they say all this months before you even start seeing each other.

It doesn't matter how you were raised, how much the one you're with hurts you, violence is not a solution. If the one you're with pushes you that far, what do you do, do you smack them, do you walk out, do you kick them out, do you try to talk it out? When your completely frustrated, what would you do? How far would you go to express yourself, or would you be able to just walk away?

Chapter 1

'The Book'

I was twenty-three, dealing in marijuana, half pound a day split between a friend and I, we will call him Mot. Mot was about twenty-two years old, had red hair and a red gotee. He was a little younger then me but out weighed me by about twenty pounds. I lived in an apartment with another friend, we will call him Kid. Kid was nineteen at this time, six feet tall, thin and was rather hyper. My pit bull was in Mot's back yard, chained to a big red dog house, his name was pilsner and he was about two years old at the time. This lasted for two months before I rented a house with Kid and his girlfriend.

Mot had a roommate, we will call him Funky. This was a funny guy, tall, over six feet three inches. He kind of had an afro, his father was the crown prosecutor in the Saskatchewan town I lived in, and he was a partier. All his party's had a theme . . . funny stuff. Funky had down loaded this book on how to build explosives, refine materials, and how to build everything from grenades, rocket propelled grenades, rocket launchers, rockets, mines, booby traps, exploding tipped bullets, exploding arrows, and details on how to break down certain components, and how to keep them safe, and how to get different types of explosives, and so much more. Some say it was the anarchist cook book, but that doesn't sound familiar, I was told this book was a step above the anarchist cook book.

I borrowed the book, on the condition I keep it safe. I sat in my room and read the book for days, twice, took notes and kept the book under my mattress. I went through it every once in a while, Funky didn't mind me having it, I was trust worthy. I moved into a house with Kid and his girl friend. I was still dealing half a pound a day in small amounts, so I was doing well financially.

I had another friend, we will call him Skinny. He was about six feet one inch, slightly taller than me. He was rather thin and had some martial arts training. I met him while driving taxi, he also worked for me when I had the delivery service, he was in a half way house and he needed a job to get out during the day. He had access to military grenades, three and a half and five pounders. He also had access to a bunch of hand guns, uzies, rifles and machine guns, a couple with silencers. I was in the process of trying to strike a deal on both cases of grenades when they were sold. So I turned my attention to the two uzies with silencers and a shoulder strap. It turned out the guns were all too expensive, but would have paid an arm and leg for those grenades.

Before I lived in the apartment with Kid, I had the upstairs of a house with my dog. In my dealings a client owed me some money, I ended up with a 357 Super Magnum hand gun, it had a nine inch barrel, it was huge. I only ever had one shell for it, but the gun said 375 calibre, so never tried to fire that shell, and people always said they could get me ammo so I wasn't worried about it. It was easy to get all kinds of toys, the problem was deciding before something better came along.

Kid was just nineteen, on the night we moved in, he got angry during a conversation about the gun in the house; he had just done four years in juvenile detention for armed robbery and was upset about the gun being in the house. My kitchen table ended up in the side of my fish tank, I was out back hitting on a young lady that had stopped by to pick up some marijuana. When I walked back in and saw the water all over, I instantly got angry and wanted to know what happened. The argument sprawled out into the front yard where there was a bunch of yelling and pushing, a group of three or four of us trying to calm him down. I walked back in the house, the tank was empty so I grab my Oscar and through him to the dogs in the backyard. Everyone came inside, we moved the broken glass to the front yard, and went back inside and drank.

The gun had to go, if I got busted and he was in the house there would be problems for him. So I agreed to take it out of town and bury it, and I did. Kid and his girlfriend moved out after about 6 months and I brought the gun home. It stayed there under my mattress with the book I got from Funky. I continued dealing in marijuana and partying. I came across a guy who wanted to trade my 357 for a 9mm Beretta. I gave him the gun and was just waiting on delivery of my 9mm when I got busted.

After a year or so in that house I decided to start my first small business, a personal delivery service. After about a month or so I was stopped at a stop sign, I had my pit bull tied up in the back of the truck. There was a cop car across the intersection and it looked like they were watching me. I went straight through the intersection, as soon as I was through the cop pulled a U-turn and came up behind me. He turned on his cherries and pulled me over. I pulled over at a gas station. They boxed me in, got out guns drawn. They couldn't get near the truck with Hatez in the back, so I stepped out, got hand cuffed, and they let me in the box of the truck to calm the dog down till the pound got there to take him.

Animal control showed up and took him and the police commenced searching the truck. They found nothing, not even a roach. They said they thought I was delivering drugs. I said heck no, was trying to quit that life and started a legitimate business to turn my life around. They let me drive away with a promise to appear. I hadn't really sold anything in almost a week, had cut down my selling share by at least half and got nailed with a full load. Two ounces of marijuana, one once of mushrooms, a set of triple beam scales, baggies, and the book I got from Funky.

I got home and the front door was booted in and the warrant, I believe, was on the door. According to the neighbours there was a swat team, maybe two, and it was fast and hard. The warrant said they were looking for a '357' or a 'BERRETTA'. The drugs and book were just a bonus, they found no weapons, there was a bb gun on the fridge, they left it behind I believe.

Funny thing is two days earlier my buddy I was trading guns with, had got busted and they were looking for a 357. He was into needles and stuff, and he figured his heat was from a different direction and stayed away from me and did not have a phone. Funny, he lived just up the block. After I got busted we made the connection and figured out what they were after, and who was behind it.

Turns out a roommate of his had an ex-girlfriend that had heard us talking, discreetly, but not enough obviously. She showed up the morning I got busted to buy some pot, but I wouldn't sell to her. She never showed up before and thought it was odd at the time. That is why the warrant didn't have drugs on it, they thought I was out. If they knew I had some, and that is what they were after, it would have been on the warrant. That day the ex-girlfriend and a friend of the neighbours' took off to go camping for the weekend. They left after she showed up at my place and before I got busted. I asked for full discloser, but the crown argued the witness feared for their life. The crowns motion was granted never did get concrete proof. In the end I got five months probation.

I owned the business for about another seven or eight months before selling it, never did get paid for it. About two months after I started the company I made the hours twenty-four hours a day. I did this for about three weeks, I almost collapsed. A couple I knew took the company over for a few days so I could recover a little. I spent the time up the block at a friend's place, the same guy that I was trading hand guns with.

I was still on edge all the time and was very stubborn in the business, with other businesses and friends. I was having serious issues with a guy who used to be a friend, we will call him Gij. He was a twenty-one year old native about five feet eleven inches tall, skinny like me. When he was out with his friends, or even just his friends there were always problems. Although I rather enjoyed the cat and mouse games, and usually ended up out driving them, I was getting tired of having to watch my back every were I went.

After a couple weeks of talking with some family in BC, I decided to sell the company and move there in about four or five months. Things were getting more tense with being in such a small town and knowing so many people and having the chip on my shoulder that I had, I was always having to out drive people, even if that meant having to drive very fast to lose them. Couldn't afford to have them follow me to a customer's house, so I did what I had to.

About a month later I found a buyer for the company, within two days I loaded my dog into the back seat, two twelve inch subs and a amp in the trunk and whatever other clothes and nic nacs I would need, stuffed into a 1988 VW Fox four door and hit the highway west to Vernon BC. I am not a materialistic person, so walking away from stuff is easy, I left behind everything, furniture, TV, bed, tons of stuff. Now the reason I left Saskatchewan and headed for BC is for another chapter. However, the things I learned from that book have always fascinated and stuck with me.

CHAPTER 2

'EARLY CHILDHOOD'

From my earliest memories there was always screaming and fighting. My father beat my mother for twenty years, and me from as young as I can remember till I stopped talking to him when I was sixteen or so, that was twenty years ago. I remember my parents going skiing in the mountains, mom coming back with a broken arm, I believe, and a banged up face with a black eye, they said she ran into a tree. I have another short memory of standing on the lawn with dad and three or four of my brothers and sisters and we watched mom walk down the road with her suit cases packed and thrown out of the house. She got a block away, we were all upset, in disbelief, confused, and so much more I am sure. After a couple more seconds dad asked us if we wanted our mother back, we all screamed yes, and he said go get her then, and we did. We were living on the island if I remember correctly, so I would have been bout seven or eight years old I figure.

We were still on the island and living in a two story house with a cottage out back. One morning my brother and I had taken a wagon wheel each from the cupboard. In the afternoon mom noticed some missing and my brother and I were standing on the back porch on the side of the house. It was on the second floor, the stairs ran all the way down along the outside of the house. When mom approached and asked if we had taken the wagon wheels, dad was in the driveway doing something and heard her ask. Even then I was scared of getting in trouble of any sort, punishment was always physical. I instinctively denied my mom's accusation, my brother told the truth and said 'Yes we did, don't you remember?' And before anything else I saw my dad run for the front door, and I just started saying no, I knew he was coming to beat me and it was a tough couple of seconds before he got to me, and when he did, he did.

Our parents' separated when I was very young and memories are only of one thing. I do not know why they separated; I do not even remember the fight. I do remember waking up Christmas morning to yelling and screaming like I never heard before, or since. My mom had taken us kids to stay with a family member, I do not remember who. I remember standing in the middle of the room and watching my mom run up and down the hallway separating the living room and bedrooms crying, sobbing and in an almost uncontrollable rage. Once I was able to get a grasp of what was going on, I learned my baby brother had passed during the night. He was about six months old, and the autopsy said it was Sid's.

I am not sure when this was, I recall nothing about it. I have heard the stories though; I believe it happened out on the island. When I was younger my father took me hostage. I do not know if I was at his house, weather my folks were separated or not. All I do know is that he used a shot gun to keep the swat team in their place. From my understanding he surrendered after about eight hours. I remember nothing, but like I said heard about it many times. Don't know if I just blocked it out, or if I was too young to remember, you'd figure I would remember all the pretty lights.

Another memory of my father is when we were living in a light coloured condo; there was a ravine out back. We were in the back yard and I believe we were setting up a wet banana, slip'n slide, with our father. He asked me to go downstairs and turn on the water. I raced down the stairs, as I was just about to touch the water tap everything went black. I came to on the floor across the room. I was scared and started to cry. I ran up the stairs and outside. Dad was yelling at me to get back down there and turn it on.

I wouldn't go, he ended up smacking me a couple times, and down I went. I slowly went down the stairs, I knew something happened, no idea what, so was very cautious. Finally got down all the stairs, crept over to the tap, gave it a light tap with my finger, it seemed ok. I turned it on and ran up the stairs as fast as possible. When I got back upstairs dad was calling me a pussy and there was nothing wrong, it was just me.

About a week later dad came and apologized, he was down stairs doing something and he ended up on the floor. It turned out there was a two hundred and twenty watt wire for the dryer that wasn't connected and was just hanging out of the wall. He played it down like nothing had happened.

While living in this condo I remember mom, my oldest brother and sister and I in the kitchen, mom was the only one standing. It was breakfast time and she said when we got home there would be a surprise for us. We wanted to know what it was, she said it was something that could make us treats, and it was as tall as her, maybe taller. She said a few other things, but those are the two that I remember. All day at school I was so anxious to see this surprise.

When I got home and walked in the door, it was the last thing I could think of. Actually it never even crossed my mind, and I was so disappointed. It was my father standing in the living room. I distinctly remember how disappointed I was. I was stunned, thinking how this could have never crossed my mind. Of course being a child I was still happy to see him, but at the same time, a child shouldn't be disappointed about a parent coming home. He was in the reserves I believe.

Up till grade three or four I was an A student, things were good, no bullying. However I remember bullying a girl and it bothered me, especially what happened to her. We actually started as friends, we were neighbours. She had large red wine color patches all over her body, I do not know what it was, a birth defect, or birth marks I believe.

I was with some other friends, boys, and they were making fun of her. I joined in. We were all on bikes riding up the street, cutting her off and one of the others got to close, I don't know if she turned to sharp to miss him or he hit her front tire with his rear, but she went over the handle bars. The other boys took off; I stopped and asked if she was ok. I felt so bad; she got up on her own crying and went home. I think we were still friends after, but I never teased her again.

We were living outside of Edmonton on an acreage and coming back from church, must have been about nine years old. Dad told us before we could change we had to clean out the car. It was white station wagon with wood paneling. I remember the three oldest, my brother, oldest sister and I had to do it. My brother and I started but our sister wouldn't help. The back drivers' side door was open; her back was to the car and standing about three or four feet from the car. I was standing in front of her demanding that she help, I am not sure where exactly my brother was, but he said he saw the whole thing. I pushed her in the chest with both hands, she spun around and fell face first into the car door frame, there was so much blood from her nose, but it did not break.

The acreages drive way was like a horse shoe with a wider mouth, the house was on the inside of the shoe, about sixty feet from the bottom. By this time dad had gone into the house and put on his slippers, thankfully. He was wearing cowboy boots. When my sister went for the house I braced myself for what was to come, accident or not. He was still in his dress clothes when he came bolting out of the house in his slippers. I remember him saying some things like 'You want to hit your sister' and the beating began. I remember rolling on the ground as I was being kicked, from the car towards the house. Once we got to the house he picked me up and slammed me into the side of the house at his eye level. The house had the old stucco on it so it was a little sharp, and being in my Sunday best, the shirt was thin. He was yelling something, but I don't remember what it was. He let me go and I slid down the wall to the ground, I recall nothing else.

We lived on the acreage for about a year and a half I believe, during the summer the grass had to be cut. We were left alone all the time, and this one time I remember having to cut the grass, they were going into town and dad told us to cut it. They were gone all day, we started cutting, took turns, and took breaks. We horsed around a little but always got back to doing some cutting. In the early evening, about five in the evening, we had about ten minutes left and I was finishing up. I looked up during a push and all I saw was my dad all puffed up and steaming towards me, I stopped mowing and knew what was coming. He yelled something about how could it have taken all day to cut this, and then kicked me in the ass and it commenced.

On the acreage we had chicken coop, my brother and I had to clean the chicken coop. It had not been done since we moved in and probably a few years before. My brother and I spent a good couple weeks swinging that crap, I was about ten or eleven, and my brother was about a year younger. I do not remember dad helping much at all. There were some beatings for not going fast enough or doing enough in a certain amount of time.

There was a pond in the back area; a small creek ran to it. Dad built a dam one summer and created a bigger pond. In the winter I had a friend spend the night for a sleep over. We were told to stay off the ice and we did, till that night. My friend wouldn't listen to me and went out on the ice, sure enough he fell in, it was only waste high, but cold. I walked out a little but he was able to get himself out right away. We had no choice but to get into the house. When dad found out what happened I could see he wanted to hit me, but he didn't, there was an outside witness. That is when I realized there must be something wrong with hitting woman and children, if it was ok, it wouldn't matter who was around. I realized it, but wasn't able to make the connection between that and my actions towards my siblings.

From the acreage we moved to a little town about one hour outside of Edmonton were my parents bought a house. I am not sure what happened exactly but once we moved to that town I was the weakling, always picked on, pushed into a wall my first day of grade seven for drinking out of the fountain, still got the bump over twenty years later. Just a reminder I guess. I had a lot of problems in that town, I remember out biking three classmates on a bike way too big for me, and getting off, and pulling that bike through a thick brush with trees about half a square block. I got out the other side and going again before they seen me, I was always fast.

I believe we lived in this town for about two years before my mom left him. I remember one morning pouring the kids corn flakes, my brother started to scream and yell that I had more; next thing dad comes flying out of his bedroom and picks me up, shakes me and throws me across the table and into the wall. It was just a regular occurrence.

There are many, many more stories like these, and I have forgotten more of them then I remember I am sure. But this is not about that, a lot of people have things in their childhood that are worse, and that psychology say can cause a person to go this way or that way. It is a matter of which way do you go, left? Right? How far left or right before you can't live with yourself or what you have done? Where is the line? Do you know?

Just because you were raised a certain way, or with certain points of view, does that make them right? We each have that voice inside that tells us what the right thing to do is, it's a matter of falling into what you have experienced because it's easier, what you want, not need, or just foolish pride gets in the way. It is hard to go against your feelings, past behaviours and peer pressures from people we think are our friends. Again, we all have the choice of which path to take, and there are only two, right and wrong, not left or right.

As you see from my childhood, I was raised it was alright to hit a woman, that when a child misbehaved a smack or twist of the ear, a kick to the butt was ok. However as an adult I have never laid a hand on a woman, or a child, I remember being on the receiving end and didn't like it. So why would I put another human being through that? Would you? We all have that choice. Even if you come from a good home, parents never divorced, good life style and loving family when you were younger, does that mean you won't become lazy, abusive or selfish? Does it mean you will never get divorced? Will you become an addict? It doesn't matter what your childhood or past was like; it is not an excuse for behaving badly in future relationships.

Unfortunately monkey see, monkey do. I was rather harsh with my brothers and sisters, especially the two older ones. I can't expect them to forgive me; I haven't been able to forgive my father so how can I expect them to forgive me. It is a choice they must make, like me, when to forgive.

I remember rather little about it actually, but the memories I do have are violent. When you are the one dishing it out, and it happens so often it becomes second nature and the brain doesn't seem to remember it as well. When you are on the receiving end it stands out. I know this, and have for many years; I have let them travel their own roads with little involvement from me.

I do have tons of little memories of hitting, kicking and beating them myself. They actually haunt me every once in a while. I have dealt with the fact that I can't go back and change it, all I can do is not repeat the cycle, but it's been hard. If there was anything I could say or do to help them, I would. However, it is a cross road they must come to. When our parents split I was worse toward my siblings, it was a rotten way to behave. I was the one always yelling and hitting them. We lived up north for a while; I was a loser in school up there also. I used what I was taught to discipline my siblings, it was wrong, but what can I do now?

CHAPTER 3

'MOVING NORTH'

I woke up that morning for school, it was quiet. Went up stairs and the folks still weren't home. I was about eleven years old. I had to get the older ones up and off to school. I had to miss school again to stay home with the smaller two. Got them off and that was that. After a bit I got a phone call, it was mom, and I could tell something was wrong.

She said she was sending a taxi for us, she was in Edmonton so I had about one hour to pack for all the kids, clothes mostly, one or two toys each only. She also said she was calling the school to get the other three sent home. Kids got home and helped pack, it was a van that pulled up to pick us up.

We stayed in Edmonton in a shelter for a while, and then we ended up in a city in northern Alberta. We stayed in a woman's abuse center for about a month or two before we found an apartment in a town where my mom was raised. We stayed in the apartment for about six months I believe before we moved into the trailer park. One day dad showed up and surprised everyone, I remember mom having a look of fear, but cannot picture it.

During this time my mom was drinking a lot and was out all the time, leaving me in charge. One night she ran through a stop sign on the highway, hit the ditch then hit a pole. The pole hit the middle of the front bumper, thankfully, two feet to the left or right and she would have hit the transformer behind it. The cross traffic saw her coming and slowed down so as not to T-bone her.

She was banged up badly. I remember that evening. She was so drunk she could barely walk; I remember thinking I should push her down and take the keys and hide the car from her. I didn't, and it haunted me for the longest time. It was a hard time for all of us, but we made it thru. She cut back on her drinking for a bit and spent all her time playing bingo instead.

She was working at the bar in town for a while, and then went to work in the next town at a bar. At first that left me in charge, which was a lot, but when my step dad met my mom things did change and there was more adult supervision. We will call him Bear. Bear was only six years older than me, heavy set about six feet tall.

She met my step dad out there, and he was able to change things, it took a bit but she cut back on the drinking massively. The marijuana started to make an appearance at this time, or maybe I just started to notice it at this time. She wasn't out as much and he was excellent with us, used to play with us all the time. We lived in a trailer park and there was an abandoned house a block away and we used to play war there all the time.

We had moved into a brand new house, it came from the olympics on the coast. The basement was built and the house was trucked in. It had two floors. When you walked in there were stairs going up and down. At the top, if you went left you were in the hallway leading to the bathroom and three bedrooms. If we went straight you were in the kitchen, if you went right you were in the living room. At the bottom of the stairs there was a door to the right. It was a fully opened basement that had a washer and dryer, and my brother got the far side, and I got the side with the door.

It was my brothers twelfth birthday, I thought it would be fun to get him drunk. Step dad and mom partied at the house by this time so there was tons of alcohol. Over a week I took about one litre of vodka and rye, about six to eight beers and stole smokes all week long from packs so they wouldn't notice.

On his birthday mom went to work and Bear drove her. Not sure when we, I guess, I started drinking that night but I was looped. I do remember sitting outside the bathroom door, drunk, and my brother was trying to get me up and down stairs so he could clean up before they got home. I convinced him to leave me alone if I gave him my beer. He just wanted me to stop. I gave him the beer and they left me alone. As soon as they were gone I pulled another out of my pocket and drank it.

The next thing I remember is laying on my bed, pretending to sleep when they got home and checked on us. The next day mom searched my room for evidence of some thing; they said they could tell I was drunk, I don't remember seeing them. Out of everything all she found was one smoke in my sock drawer, but it was enough.

Over the course of the next year I took apart a pizza cutter and used the wheel as a throwing star. Add a couple darts and I was winging them around the basement. The basement wasn't painted; it was all bran new drywall. There were tens of thousands of holes and marks all over, not one piece was spared the destruction. I took a hatchet and dug a hole into the concrete floor. Not all the way threw, but far enough. I used the hatchet to smash numerous walkmans, calculators anything that was there.

My classmates called it 'Gleeking'; it is when you use pressure with your tongue to shot saliva out the side of your mouth. My classmates spit on me all the time. In this town, in this school you were not allowed to go home for lunch, but a few times I did because they spit on my lunch. I was always tripped, pushed, spit on, harassed one way or another every day. I thought about suicide, but wasn't my thing. Even back then I knew I am not going alone.

I stole forty dollars from my mom's wallet and hitch hiked eight hours to Edmonton. My first ride was a school bus. When they picked me up I knew I could be in trouble, I was supposed to be in school. They asked me where I was headed and I told them my mom and I were traveling down from a northern town and I was asleep in the back, I woke up we were at a service station, got out to use the washroom.

When I came out she was gone. Was hitching to Edmonton because I knew where they were going. It didn't look like they really believed me, but they took me for about forty minutes.

When they dropped me off they were very hesitant, but I insisted. There I was on the side of the highway with my thump out again. Two rather large ladies in a small grey four door sedan pulled up. The back seat was full of clothes, paper and stuff, but I hoped in. Don't remember what we talked about and I believe they got me to the half way point. From there I spent the forty on a bus ticket to Edmonton, bought a sandwich and got on the bus.

When I got there I called home to let them know I was ok. So there I was, about thirteen years old, in the bus terminal in Edmonton, hungry with no money. There was an A+W restaurant in the bus station and I went in with the last of my change. I tried to order the smallest burger, still didn't have enough. I talked to the manager, even at that age I could deal with people, he was a very nice guy, and paid the difference. I got a glass of water with it. After I walked around, I thought I really didn't think this threw, now I am here, I am not going home, eight hundred kilometres from home, not even money left for the phone.

I was just sitting there, looking around, thinking about what I was doing or going to do. Had been here for a couple hours and wait, that guy looks familiar. He sees me and starts to come my way; he is walking like he is in a rush. Oh ya, it's one of my uncles on my dad's side. He sat down and talked a bit, in the end he took me home and let me spend the night. After talking again it was decided I had no choice but to go home. I spent a couple days there then took the bus back home. I believe my uncle paid for the ticket to help my mom out. When I got home it was the same old same old. It was a combination of school problems and home issues that I took off, I really didn't care, just wanted out. Things got worse for me and I was harsher with my siblings. I got expelled from school and went to live with my father.

My step dad was a god sent at that exact time and to boot he was only a few years older than me, so he was still a kid at heart, but it didn't change me enough to stop hitting my brothers and sisters. Also didn't change being bullied, it got worse, I eventually got expelled from school and wanted to live with my father. I knew what I was in for, but I would have no siblings around, I thought it was worth it, still don't know if it was the right choice or not, but for my siblings, I am sure it was. The beatings started immediately, but it was just me so I had more alone time. I lived there for about six to eight months I think before I had to get away from him.

I was about fifteen when I moved in with my father. We lived on the third floor of an apartment building. There were a time or two we had to go to northern Alberta to pick up my brothers and sisters, once we went all the way to Salmon Arm, BC. I remember once we were on the highway, I had my learners permit and was driving. This mid 1980's Chevy truck came up behind us with its bright lights on. My father was in the passenger seat and when the truck went to pass he told me to floor it.

I was driving a 1979 ford LTD II with a 351 Windsor, green in colour with all the kids in the car. The truck was unable to pass us. I was very nervous; we had hit 130km/h that time. It happened a few more times, but dad was yelling at me and the kids were loud and I didn't have a lot of driving experience at the time. The truck tried one last time and gave it hell, dad was really yelling and we ended up hitting just over 160km/h before the truck got tired and pulled over to put some room between us.

Although it was kind of nice having them around once in a while I liked the fact they had to go home. Life wasn't much better living with him. I was still a scrawny white kid in school that got picked on all the time; I even kept my mouth shut this time around. I was still just the new kid in a big city.

The whole time I lived with him, he kept rear ending people. This was about six years after mom left him and turns out he had been on valume the whole time. So he was addicted to them plus he drank, he could be rather unpleasant. It wasn't long before I had to move out.

My mom and step dad said I was to violent toward the others to move back home; I ended up moving in with my uncle Jerry, who has since passed on. I was there for about a year I think, and then I was allowed to move back home. Although living there was rather strict, it wasn't physical. Had to do something like two hours of home work a day and if there wasn't I had to just sit and study. He said two things to me that stuck, and because of these two things I have started so many business and tried so many different things . . . . 1—The only stupid question is the one you don't ask . . . 2—If you don't ask the question, the answer is automatically no, what have you got to lose?

CHAPTER 4

'PARTY TIME'

I was sixteen, living in Edmonton, back at home with the family, we called it 'Giovanni's'. It was a corner lot with a Safeway and mini mall across the street. I had dropped out of school a couple months earlier and was doing nothing with my time but hanging out with friends. I was stealing smokes from my folks and when it came out that I was smoking I got kicked out. My buddy, Nutso was about a year younger than me, slightly taller, dark hair that was medium length. He got kicked out of his place the same day, I don't remember why. Nutso had a friend named Paul. He was A-wall from the youth detention center, about the same build as Nutso, but had short black hair. We all hung out for about three months.

We spent the first night in the park, maybe even the second. We were both working, so we lied about our age and got an apartment together. It was party time and what a party it was. Nutso and I were working at a pizza place making pizzas. During our breaks we went out back and kicked the hell out of each other, there was just never enough time to finish, young and full of energy. This went on for months and we always went back to work bloody and banged up, after an eight hour shift and two or three breaks. Ouch.

I was closing one night at the pizza store across town, Nutso, Paul, another guy and two girls showed up in a red Chevy S-10 to pick me up. I had a bad feeling, so I said I was only getting in if I was driving, I didn't even have a license at the time. I drove directly to our side of the city, on the way I learned the truck was stolen.

Once back on our side of the city, Nutso insisted he wanted to drive again, I sat on the passenger side with one of the girls sitting on my lap, boney butt let me tell you. His driving was totally erratic; I couldn't take it anymore and had to get out. The other guy in the truck thought it would be fun to ride in the back, I told him not to, he would definitely get hurt, something was going to happen. After a little convincing he got back in the cab of the truck.

I started to walk up the block and just as I got around the corner I heard the motor rev and them peel out. Then the revs came down but the sliding tire sound was still there, after a second or two I heard a loud smash. I kept walking. Then the truck came around the block and up to me, it was wobbling rather badly. Everyone was rattled and anxious to get out of the truck. Just as they pulled up to me a car came flying out of the alley looking at the truck, he drove by slowly and left.

When they reached me, I was shaking my head and the guy who wanted to ride in the back thanked me. Turns out after they pinned it they tried to take a corner, half way into it the back end started to slide. It hit the curb with such force the truck bounced up at least two feet and bounced back into the middle of the street. Again, buddy thanked me. We ditched the truck and spent the next few hours walking around, and got home around ten in the morning.

Nutso and Paul stole a car one night; I refused to get in because I thought they would get caught, just brought too much attention to themselves. They were tired later that night and stopped at a school parking lot to catch some sleep. Not the smartest place to park. They woke up to cops and got arrested. That was the end of that apartment, he lost his job and I couldn't afford it myself. I ended up moving back in with the family.

Mom had moved from Giovanni's and was living further west in a condominium complex. I moved back in with the family, I had run of the whole basement, I had most of the furniture from the apartment. I just started smoking pot and could not roll joints and did not have a pipe. I met this girl at the corner store, very attractive girl, we will call her Boll. About five feet eight inches tall, long blond hair, large breast's and a butt that didn't quit. She had a friend with her, but wasn't really looking at her. I asked if they wanted to smoke a joint. She said no but I would like her brother and we should meet. So we walked back to her house.

She lived in a different condo complex about two blocks away. Unlike ours, which used all three floors, theirs was above and below. They lived on the lower one and had a back yard. We walked up to the gate; it was a dark brown, like the fence and trim around the building. The yard was small and two or three steps we were in the house. I had just gotten my last pay check from the pizza place, it was worth about twenty dollars, one part time shift. I had no bank account at the time and no way to cash it. There were also tensions at home, I do not remember why exactly, I think it was because I quit my job and wasn't in school.

When I walked into the house, we entered on the right side of the living room, directly across in the corner was her mother in a chair, a couch to her right had a girl with red hair, we will call her Red. She was very attractive. The brother was sprawled out on the floor, we will call him Bud. He had blond hair, heavy set and a little stubble on his face; he was about six months older than me. His grandmother and a native fellow, we will call him Disturbed, were sitting at the dining room table smoking. Disturbed had black hair, was very thin, but crazy. Never seen him lose a fight or back down from anyone.

If you criss crossed the living room, there were three stairs, at the top if you went left you would end up down stairs. If you went forward ten feet you would enter the hall to the front door and grandma's room. To the right was the open dining room with a small kitchen on the other side. The dining room was about two feet higher than the living room, separated by a hand rail. Other than that it was an open room.

Once intros were made the conversation immediately went to the check and my needing to move out, all of a sudden her brother came alive. He bounced off the floor and asked how much the cheque was worth. He said I could move in if I bought a case of beer, I said if I could cash it I would. He said to leave that to him, then went and talked to his grandmother and she cashed it.

We immediately went to buy a case of beer, I moved in that day. I had bought the beer, which was considered rent, they let me have the bedroom, I actually hadn't met everyone yet, and so was lucky I got the bedroom. It turns out there were three bedrooms, two down stairs and one upstairs. His mother and grandmother shared a room. His sister had one because she was a couple years younger, didn't look like it, and was still in school.

To get downstairs there were three steps down to a landing, then a right on the landing took you down to the basement hall way. At the bottom of the stairs it was a quick right, the first door on the left was the sisters' room, I got the next room to the left. At the end of the hallway was the washroom, on the right across from my room there was a door to a large room with a washer and dryer. It was the party room and had tons of room. It had its own access door to the outside, so we could come and go as pleased and we did.

In the end there were the four family members, Grandma, Mother, Bud, and Boll. Bud had also moved in some others and all they did was party, Red, Disturbed and one more other guy, we will call him Blondie, he was older then all of use by a couple years, long blonde hair going bald on top. With me that was eight people living in a three bedroom condo and the five of us partied seven days a week. Boll was still a little young and partied with us once in a while.

Again, I was an easy target, three beers and I couldn't walk, I was a light weight. Bud had a friend that lived next door; he hauled carpet for a living so we will call him Lifter. He was shorter, about five feet five inches and was very strong. He used to sell us bags of shake, about a half ounce for thirty dollars. One way or another we bought a sixty of black velvet and a bag of pot every day. We partied hard for months there. I had met this girl, we will call her Stacey, I was sixteen years old. We dated for about four months. She had an STD so we never slept together. After a couple months I went to the doctor's office to get checked just in case. The doctor barely spoke english, he said I had herpes. How the hell was that possible, I didn't even sleep with her!

Stacey and I were helping my mom move; she was in the back of the truck and insisted that I help her out of the truck. She did it with attitude so I walked away and took another load in. When my mom came out she asked Stacey to help and she told my mom she was pregnant, it was mine and not to tell me. Well mom did tell me and the relationship ended shortly after. I never slept with her.

We used to do a lot of LSD back then also. One Christmas we were all flying high and disturbed overdosed, it happened at Bud's house in the back, outside. Bud had a bunch of family down that year. While he was in the back overdosing and blacking out we were all trying to calm him down. When he looked up he saw me, said the word DAD! He grabbed me and tossed me around like a rag doll. I ended up being thrown about six feet, I was in pain and when I got up, I ran to Lifter's for help.

He went running out ahead of me, he approached Disturbed all friendly like, once he got close enough he put Disturbed in full nelson. I went running through Bud's backdoor and in front of his family I yelled 'Disturbed has over dosed', and fell flat on my face. One of the neighbours must have called the emergency services; we could hear the sirens getting closer. Once the paramedics got there they stayed away until back up arrived, but Disturbed had stopped breathing, Lifter could not let go in case he came to and started to freak out again. So while he still had him in the full nelson, Lifter set Disturber's chest down on the sidewalk. He pushed his chest into the ground to try to get his heart going again; it must have worked because he started to spas' out again.

Soon after police and fire fighters showed up, in the end one ambulance, two fire trucks and a ton of cops showed up. It took eight of them to hold down Disturbed while they hand cuffed him to the bed. The rest of us hid down stairs the rest of the night. He survived, and it started all over the next day when he got home.

My mom had just gotten me a job working with her at a truck stop. She was a cashier and I was in the back as assistant cook. We worked the same hours so it was great for commuting. I worked there for about three months while living with Bud's family and friends. In the room I got, there were three benches about seven feet long. Like I said I was a light weight, I would pass out after a couple hours, or I would go to bed early for work. I woke up a few times with toothpaste in my hair. One time they took a bic pen, emptied the ink into a lid of same sort and found a pipe about 1.5 inches in diameter. They dipped the pipe and put circles all over my face. When I woke up for work, I scrubbed and scrubbed, but it was still there.

I ended up moving the benches, so I slept on two and used the third to put one end against the door and the other side up against the two I was sleeping on. It would stop them from coming in and I would feel it when they did. They thought that was clever, and just pounded on the door to wake me up instead. Once in a while they climbed in threw the window and got me.

I ended up moving back home, I was going to lose my job, needed a quite place to sleep. I had bought a fridge while I was living with Bud. And when we moved it into the basement at moms, it became the party place. Bud had met my parents, they liked him, and he was a good guy. Blondie and Disturbed were loud and violent but Bud was good at controlling their behaviour, to a big degree. Hard to deal with a drunk, when you are drunk. This went on for a while.

We partied for a few years like that. Bud got a job with Lifter; the company Lifter worked for did alcohol deliveries at night. They needed drivers so about two weeks before I turned eighteen the company put me through a driving course to get my license. Got it the day I turned eighteen and started doing deliveries that night.

We worked there for about a year or so. We rented an apartment together and the party continued. We both quit at the same time, tired of getting a two week pay check worth two hundred dollars. The boss put a stop payment on the pay checks which we cashed at money mart. In the end money mart sued us and we were responsible to pay back half the money.

Shortly after Bud and his family moved to Saskatchewan. I had bought a car and was doing deliveries for a pizza place. My family had moved to southern Alberta and I moved in with Lifter. During this time I realized I needed to have some sort of plan for the future. I loved to drive and wanted to travel, figured the best thing to do without having to go back for my grade twelve was to get my class 1a license, and I did. No matter where I move or live I should always be able to find work. I was nineteen at the time.

A couple months after getting the class 1a license I was tired of Edmonton, insurance had run out on my car and I wasn't working any more. I made arrangements and caught the bus to southern Alberta were the rest of my family was. I spent about a month sleeping in the living room before I found a job. I never had a problem looking for work; I am not picky and have done many different kinds of jobs and in different fields.

I got a job working for a company out of California. They come to Canada during the summer months to do paving for farmers drive ways. It paid one hundred dollars minimal a day and the company paid for the hotel room. Had to buy our on food, I got tired of eating out all the time so ended up getting a kitchenette to save money.

While we were in Calgary I went to a bar one night after work. I was sitting there bored out of my mind and noticed this lady also sitting by herself. She was dressed in a black out fit with a skirt; she was a few years older than me, blond, about five feet seven inches tall. I offered to buy her a drink, she accepted and we sat together and talked. We ended up back at her place and while we were there I had to tell her about my medical condition. It was a hard thing to bring up and talk about, after all, I was only in town for a little while and she didn't know what hotel I was in, so I didn't have to tell her.

I could have just slept with her and kept my mouth shut but my conscience would not let me. We hung out every night after work for a week. She had just broken up with her boyfriend and he took all of her money so her power got disconnected. She said she had a cheque coming in a couple days, so I offered to lend her the hundred, she had a child, and they needed power. She was very reluctant, but I made her take it. She swore to pay it back, I wasn't worried about it at the time, and it was a day's pay.

After about five days of knowing each other and lending her the money, she said as long as we use a condom she was ok with it. I could see in her eyes she was still not sure. In the end we never did sleep together, I just couldn't do it with her eye's saying otherwise. She paid back the money, and we left town a few days later, I knew her for about eight days, never to see again.

We moved every week or two to a new town or city. During this time I had made contact with Bud in Saskatchewan, he had come to work with us for a bit, but one of the workers they brought up from the United States was a loud mouthed, inconsiderate, pushy and conniving Texan. I had a hard enough time working with him, but Bud lasted two days.

That night we were drunk and in Calgary at a cowboy bar. They had just gotten into a fight and Bud was steamed and couldn't take it anymore. He packed his stuff and as we were headed to the highway so he could hitch hike back home, he asked if he could have my shoes, his had holes. He had a long trip, so I gave him my shoes and watched him walk away at about two in the morning, drunk, down the highway.

I got a hold of him a couple days later, turns out he was blacked out, by the time he woke up, he was in a semi headed west. He couldn't piece together what happened that night, especially the shoes. He thought he stole them from me. He had to turn around and hitch hike back to Saskatchewan from the other side of the Rocky Mountains. It was kind of funny. I had to explain to him what happened that night. He just didn't understand how he woke up in a semi truck headed west with my shoes.

The plan was when I got laid off in the fall to move to Saskatchewan, I was supposed to save some money to insure a truck that Bud had when I got there. The company had a family emergency and had to head back to California. I was only twenty years old and wasn't allowed to drive the truck in the United States so I decided to stay in Canada. I drove the truck to the boarder, we got there about three in the morning, and we left the truck, trailer, equipment and all my stuff on the Canadian side and went over the border to the nearest town. We got up about seven that morning to go back to take care of the paper work so they could cross back into the US. When all was said and done I was standing on the US side with two large duffle bags, one suit case and a stereo.

I walked into the US customs building and they wanted to search my stuff. They found an old pill bottle wrapped in black electrical tape, and three packs of papers. They ended up strip searching me and calling in the police. They hauled me back into the US about thirty minutes to the closest court house. I saw the judge in a room no bigger than a typical office. I was given ten days in jail or pay a three hundred and sixty dollar fine. It was Thanksgiving weekend and spending three or four months on the road I wanted the turkey dinner and didn't want to do any time in the United States. After I paid the fine they told me the jail was just built and there was only one other person in it, figures, I would have done the time had I known that.

When the company left they paid me four hundred dollars cash as a final pay check. Living on the road, I drank every night and didn't save any money, all I had was the money they gave me, and minus the fine I was left with forty dollars. I was out of smokes so I bought a cartoon of Marlboro's and headed for the Canadian side. The Canadian side was much more pleasant, they thought it was awfully stupid to charge me with that, but that is Canada for you. After I got through there, I was stuck in the town at the border. I called my mom's and told them what happened, Bear said he would come and get me; I said I would be at the hotel bar playing pool. It would take him about two hours to get to me so I went for a jug of beer and a game of pool.

He showed up and picked me up. I had no money left so we talked about me staying with them till I could get back on my feet; he said no problem and I moved in. I was there for about two or three months before I found a job. I ended up working at a school as a general labourer and had to put moving to Saskatchewan on hold. After about a month of work I got a place with my brother and a friend, called Ren. He was a burly kind of guy, heavy set, deep voice, blonde hair and a couple years older than me. Kind of looked like the lead singer of Metallica. We partied hard in that house. My brother was still going to school and Ren had a job somewhere.

My brother was drinking more; we had to pass the police station to walk home from the bar. He would sneak into the parking lot and steal the plates off the cars. Then bring them home and throw them in the attic, there were about half a dozen up there when we moved out. He didn't last long in school with all the drinking he was doing. It ended up causing a lot of issues between us and made things rough when he dropped out and mom paid his rent.

In the first month we had a house warming party. That night Ren slept with my girlfriend because I wouldn't leave the party I was hosting. I borrowed this really loud house stereo from a friend at work. I was in southern Alberta, about nine or ten months, I had dated a few girls from the school. It was a school for students that dropped out and couldn't or didn't want to go back to a high school. I dated a girl that partied a lot, one night we went to the bar, it was about ten at night and I had to go home for work in the morning. She stayed at the bar and drank with her friends.

The next morning at work the teachers were asking where she was, I told them I had no idea, I went home and she stayed, she was over eighteen she can make her own decisions. After this the teachers blamed me for her no shows, the relationship ended shortly after that.

The last girl I dated knew I was leaving town in a couple weeks, but let me move in until then. She was about five feet three inches tall, size double D breasts and deadly eye's. She also had two kids. My brother started to date her best friend. One morning I woke up and went up stairs and sat on the couch. My brother's girlfriend came up from the spare bedroom and then her ex-boyfriend came up the stairs.

My girlfriend took me aside and asked me to keep quite. I said I couldn't, but would hold off to give her the chance to tell my brother, but it had to be that day. She didn't and I had to tell him a couple days later. He was pissed at me for a long time for not telling him right away and he was right, I felt terrible. After that I had no respect for my girlfriend or her friends and was happy to be leaving and going to Saskatchewan. When my unemployment insurance cheques started coming in, I moved.

Chapter 5

'Saskatchewan'

I was on unemployment when I moved out to Saskatchewan. I moved into the place where Bud was staying, they were called the chicken coups. It was just a long building with about twelve dwellings; each had a front and back door. There were about six to seven of us living in this two bedroom place. It was a serious party every night. After a month or so Bud and I moved in next door. Our buddy Mot moved in and slept on the couch.

The first week I moved up there, I met this girl, we will call her Oops, she wasn't attractive but I wanted human contact. We didn't sleep together that night, I had told her about my medical issue and she thought I was lying to her but I must of made an impression because she stalked me for years afterward, even if she had a boyfriend.

The first month Bud and I were in our place, Oops found out where I lived and came by. We were partying at our place and Oops went next door and asked some of our female friends if I had herpes or if I was I just lying so I didn't have to have sex with her. Well, I had only been in town for a couple months so of course no one knew. The female friends approached me and asked if it was true. I was given a way out when they thought it was just because I wouldn't sleep with her. I am not a liar and the seconds I stood there, they had their answer and they made sure everyone knew within hours.

After a couple more months, I ended up dating this other girl, her name was Jen. She was about five feet tall, long dark slightly curly hair. We were parting at our place one day with a bunch of friends. My girlfriend was sitting on a friend's lap, his girlfriend walked in and screamed in front of everyone "What are you letting her sit on your lap for? You want to catch herpes!" I was standing behind her coming in from the other room. I went outside and was looking for something to hit. I was wearing a black pair of cowboy boots and started kicking a fence in.

The boyfriend came out to talk and apologized for her. We talked for a bit, he wasn't the kind of guy you said no too. He was a little under six feet but had the muscle and attitude to get what he wanted. Tattoo's all over and stacked. He spent most of his life bouncing in and out of prison, his name was Ike. She came and apologized but it was too late, there was no going back after that. I was so pissed off. Some of the girls in our group did nothing but cause problems for me with that information; I held a grudge against some of them for a long time.

Oops would show up at our parties, most of the time with a boyfriend for appearances but when they weren't around she was all over me. Over the next two or three years she was always trying to get with me. Everyone could see it and tried to help me escape many times, but hard to out fox someone when your drunk and it is the middle of the night.

About a year and a half after I met Oops, I was single again and one night I was very drunk at a party, could hardly walk. She ended up showing up and said she would walk me home, I tried to get out without her, but was too drunk to argue about it anymore or stumble away fast enough. We got about a block away and I fell, was tripped, I don't remember. We were lying on someone's grass under a tree. She wanted to have sex, I didn't, plus we had no condoms. That was my excuse and tried to stick with it. After about fifteen minutes she got her way and we had sex on someone's front lawn at like three in the morning. I felt bad for a few years after that.

We partied all the time, so much so I ended up in the hospital for malnutrition. We had come across thousands of dollars of meat in an illegal manner, different types of steaks, chicken, veal, ham and some roasts. It is all I ate for about three or four months. I would get up in the morning, throw a couple steaks on, use the washroom come out flip them. It was a morning ritual. All we ate was meat for months, and drank a lot of beer and vodka. The meat fed about twelve people for almost four months, there was a lot. It took two cars to haul it all away, with about eight people loading, it was nuts and very risky behind a hotel.

I had gotten a job finally, driving a dump truck. In the first week I was going to bed earlier to get up in the morning, well my roommate brought a party home during the week and there was too much noise to sleep. I ended up staying up all night. I was so angry I punched out a couple windows and was bleeding all over. We had no band aids so I used toilet paper and scotch tape to cover it up. When it came time for work I was beat, but I went.

It was an hour drive to the job and I fell asleep, stinking like booze. When we got to the site and they woke me up, I noticed my home made bandages didn't work and got blood all over his truck, he was not happy. I worked my shift, got home and got fired. I ended up finding a job driving a taxi for a private owner. I worked the night shift, I was up all night any ways and it would stop me from drinking so much.

After a while we, Bud, Mot and I moved into an apartment building. We dealt a little pot, when we weren't working, which was a lot, we were on social services and playing video games all night. We lived like pigs, showering maybe a couple days a week, dishes got done when someone visiting got disgusted and washed them. Same with the bathroom, no way any of us guys were going to clean it. Once in a while, when it got bad, we would pay some girl to clean up, but they usually did it for free. Eventually we just hired maids at ten dollars an hour, and they only had an hour if they wanted to get paid.

One Christmas, we bought a Texas Mickey of Black Velvet. We sat at the table; four of us sat at the table and drank till it was gone. A few people stopped and had a drink, but we drank most of it. I do not remember much, but the one guy drank so much he puked under the table. No one could deal with it so we turned the table upside down to cover it up. It stayed like that for about a week, when it was all dry we lifted the table off, wiped it and vacuumed the floor, back to the usual, drinking, but now we had our table back.

I just got laid off from some job and was waiting for my unemployment to start. I was broke and waiting for my cheque, after two months so I broke into a convenience store to steal smokes and got busted. I ended up getting ten days for a previous fine for drinking in public, actually walking down the street in front of the police station. While I was in there I figured if the government is paying I am getting my medication.

Since the day I was diagnosed with herpes nothing had changed. I spent a fortune on the medication and there was never any improvement. I was under the understanding there were soars, you were itchy, lots of discomfort, but I never had those symptoms. How was I to know, I was just a sixteen year old kid and he was a doctor. When I went to see the doctor, I was almost twenty-three when I went to see another doctor, this time; I was told I was clean. I asked a bunch of questions, he spoke perfect English. I was stumped, flabbier gasped and realized I was going to have to track down Oops.

When I got out and back to the apartment, it took me about a week to track down Oops. Two of my friends were there when I made that call. I asked if she caught anything from me, she said no, she thought I was lying to her again. When I hung up the phone I was in total disbelief, but at the same time I was relieved and furious. Relived that I was clean but so angry after the last six or seven years of rejection, insults and comments made by other people over the years. All the times I had to have that conversation with the opposite sex, it was so hard, so belittling, and turns out totally unnecessary.

The group I was hanging with were not pansies. Evan was five feet ten inches tall with dark short hair. Stalky had been taught by his grandfather how to box, he was a golden glove champ. Evan lived with Ike at this time and Ike's brother was three times the size of Ike, a weight lifter and held a couple records. Ike was under half his size but he was in and out of jail his whole life and was the toughest of us all.

He was very untrustworthy, stole from many of us but he wasn't the kind of guy you would want to charge or go after, he would hammer you even if he was in the wrong.

I ended up buying a taxi from the company I was working for; I borrowed a thousand dollars off a friend for the down payment. I was working ten to twelve hours a day, five shifts a week. I tried to get my friend Gij a job but he ended up getting his license and taking off. He said he passed his security clearance and when he got his licence that I paid for, he was gone.

I moved in with a guy I met at work, his name was Dekoc. I met him driving taxi, he drove for the company. He was in his late thirties and I needed a place to live so he let me rent a bedroom downstairs. I was working nights, until about six in the morning, one early afternoon in the first week, he was upstairs making a ton of noise. I got up and went upstairs to see what was going on. There were two of his friends there and they were all getting high on crack. I walked in as they were lighting up and his friends, all tweaked out, started make a massive problem for me. They said I was a nark because I looked familiar; they wanted to know who I was and see my I.D. immediately. I recognized them from past cab rides.

Dekoc just looked at me and said "These are my friends and I trust them". So I had to get my driver's license and show it to them to avoid a fiscal altercation. The license made no difference; it was what you would expect from tweakers. They started to tweak out all the time, all day, while I was trying to sleep. They got louder and louder over the days, they made it very clear I had to move out. I paid about four hundred dollars for rent but had to move out within about one week. I stayed with friends for a couple weeks to save some money and went to live in a hotel kitchenette.

After about eight months the company seized my car because they said I wasn't working enough. The guy who lent me the money to buy the taxi was frustrated with them also and ended up putting the owner threw a piece of glass on a display case, he was a big guy, full beard and had a knack for falling asleep behind the wheel. He had been with the company for years. I was actually working more than the average day driver. I had the chance to get out of my contract so I took it and walked away from the company.

After this I was so discouraged at everything, just life in general. I just lost my first small business; I started drinking more and was just starting to deal marijuana. I had paid back most of the down payment that I borrowed to get the taxi. He had seen that my other buddy, Mot could sell a ton of the pot, so I became the middle man. They didn't want to meet each other, it was funny they knew who each other were by reputation and passing by each other, but didn't want to meet. Eventually they did, but whatever.

I was moving about two pounds a week for them, then I started and it doubled. I started to party, buy stuff and was doing what you would think a dealer does but I was in it for the good time, not the flashy stuff. I started by moving into the upstairs of a house, unfortunately I was taking it over from another friend how was dealing, his name was Clyde, so the house was already heat bagged out. In the first month I acquired a beautiful, mixed, three quarters pit bull and one quarter bull masse. He was about seven months old and had a huge frame, his name was Pilsner. Mot took a female version of mine, but twenty percent smaller, however, two hundred percent more vicious. He named her Miss Piggy, after her father, Pig. I was about twenty two.

I also acquired a rather large hand gun, damn it was big. Shells were very hard to come by, never did get to fire it. Had it for about three years, I kind of miss it. I wasn't in the house long before I got a letter from an anonymous neighbour telling me they were calling the cops in a week if I didn't get out, so out I went.

I moved into an apartment with Kid and his girlfriend. I bought this big red dog house that was insulated for the dog; it went into Mot's back yard. Pilsner was tied to the fence for about two months. I lived two blocks away straight up the alley and went buy all the time, just selling pot and hanging out, getting high with Bud, Mot, Funky, Shrimp and a few others. Shrimp was younger than the rest of us and much shorter. He was a cool kid. He was just part of the group.

Funky had this out of the world home stereo, one hundred compact disc changer, two, five foot towers, one boom box, and a big amp, neighbours hated us I am sure.

I moved into this small grey house with Kid and his girlfriend. There was a double car garage with no doors, so it was completely open, and for some reason the doorways faced the house, but the back of the garage was against the alley. It was a two bedroom one bathroom house and the rent was cheap. The whole yard was dirt and we rocked that house. I over dosed on LSD, but not an overly bad kind of. It was more of a body over dose.

It was the nicest stuff I ever tried. It was so pure, such a rush and I wanted more. I waited the two days to flush my system and took two doubles. I was sitting at the kitchen table, not even fifteen minutes, come on, let's go already. All of a sudden my stomach was very upset, I stood up and dry heaved on the table, two little white drops fell out of my mouth. I wiped them up and sat in the living room.

By now I had a big TV with Sony play station, Nintendo sixty-four with four controllers and tons of games. The house stereo was a twenty-four disc changer, two, four foot towers, one boom box, one amp and tuner. In the back was my 1968 Dodge Fury III and out front was my 1980 Dodge full size, short body van. I started to look at illegal fire arms at this time a little more.

When I went and sat in the living room in my recliner, I was instantly smashed. It was the weirdest body buzz I have ever felt, I couldn't move. I sat there for over twelve hours watching TV, playing video games and watching white noise. A very sexy lady came by, I had been working on her for a while but I couldn't get up for the life of me. Other friends stopped by, I wasn't moving, it lasted for about twenty hours. I'm happy to say that I haven't touched the stuff since.

One cold winter night at about three in the morning I was sitting there playing video games and could here this dog going nuts up the street. Oh nuts, I let Pilsner out a while ago. I went to the back door, he was gone. He was chained to a fifteen inch rim and tire, with about twelve feet of chain. He had pulled it through one foot of snow all the way up the alley, then down a block and a half. As I was walking up the street I was yelling his name, Pilsner! I realized, here I am, in the middle of the night, walking up the middle of the street, in a Saskatchewan town yelling for a beer of all things, time to change his name. Found him, he had tried to go between two cars and the tire was hung up on one of them. Made him drag it back home, got him inside to warm up and changed his name to Hatez.

I was still in the six months later, I started my first small business, it was a delivery service. I had my own place, a 1984 Ford F-150, five speed, inline six cylinder, and a 1988 Volkswagen Fox in the backyard that needed brakes. Things were looking up. I was working so much and was having issues with several people in town so my road rage and frustration took on a whole new level.

By the time I started this company I was angry, everyone was going to do things my way or they would get added to the banned list, which included restaurants, friends and anyone between. I was the only delivery service in town. My road rage was terrible, I had an ex-friend, Gij, he got all his friends involved so when I went to do a delivery I had an issue of some sort at least once a day.

In the third month, I changed the hours of the company to twenty-four hours a day. That was a mistake; it lasted for about three weeks. I would sleep between deliveries whenever I could, but after three weeks I stopped it because it was killing me. I had some friends that could see what it had done to me so they agreed to take the company for a weekend so I could relax. I went across the street for the weekend and hung out with some other friends.

Well these friends of mine, although they were good guys, they were into hard drugs, needles. I was angry, frustrated and burnt out inside so I decided to try it. I liked it, it was different. I was in it for about a month before I realized this is not what I wanted in my life and quit, never to do again. I found out later a few of us, including me contracted HEP-C.

I kept working while involved in that stuff, just saved it for time off, and made sure I had time off. I always have had a work ethic, I just don't work traditional jobs, and I like being the boss. Sometimes it was nice not to have the responsibility and get a pay check though.

Over the next couple months, I was talking with family out in the Vernon, British Columbia area. They were talking about how much money they were making growing pot. If done right, they were about twenty thousand every three months, and that wasn't an overly large operation. I thought what possibilities. So I decided to move to BC, but not for about six months to let them get a better set up and me time to build company a little more and sell it.

I had owned the delivery service for about seven or eight months at this point. I was working from open to close, seven days a week again. My road rage was very bad and my temper was actually worse than it ever had been. I was so burnt out, I just didn't care anymore, and I actually took immense joy in driving completely off the wall. I am very good at identifying vehicles and in a small town they are easy to find. I knew who was following me, I just didn't have the time to mess around so had to lose them.

In the end I was so wired up and tired of stuff, I found someone to buy the company for five thousand dollars, payable to the guy I owed the money to and I was supposed to get five hundred dropped in my account within a month. I left town within forty-eight hours of making it a done deal. I packed my dog in the back seat, had two twelve inch speakers and an amp installed in the trunk and packed just the necessities in what room was left in the trunk. I left everything else, all furniture, kitchen stuff, bedroom furniture and everything else you would have in a house. I was twenty-five years old.

At this point I was ready, I had read, and studied that book two years earlier and had tons of idea's. I needed money and a place to work. I was so frustrated and tired of getting the short end of the stick; I figured taking a life would be easy. It was getting away with it that would be the hard part. To learn what I needed to, I needed money, free time and a lot of land for testing, free of people.

The only problem is that I was leaving about six months early, I only owned the company for nine months and was so fed up with it that within one month, I found a buyer that my financial backer would allow to take the debt and packed and left in record time. I was looking forward to heading west and getting a fresh start.

It was a long drive, thumping to the music. I stopped to let the dog out once in a while. On my way to Vernon I stopped to see my brother in southern Alberta. I had some front end problems with my car and got stuck there for seven days. And it turns out my second sister, child number four, had just moved from the place I was headed to. So I got the low down on what to expect. I was told that our youngest sister, half sister, was out of control. She was only about seven or eight years old and she listened to no one. I was told she was almost to the point of being physical with mom. She did what she wanted, when she wanted.

I spent five days working on my car so I could get back on the highway, finally it was done and off I went. When I got to Vernon, I got lost and had to call and get someone to meet me at a seven eleven store and followed them back to the house. I was in BC, unemployed, broke, and looking so forward to the next five years would bring. I was twenty-five years old.

CHAPTER 6

'VERNON B.C.'

When I got to BC, I ended up staying with family. I slept in the computer room when it wasn't being used but it was always being used. The whole reason I moved there, was falling apart every time, nothing was working. I wanted to get into my own place and start an operation. I wanted to start my tests, wanted to build stuff. After a couple months, I had to get a job. I ended up with a job driving taxi. I did that for about six months before I came across an owner of a taxi who wanted to sell his car. We entered into a deal. It was as close to a done deal as possible but when the car went for its safety, it failed miserably and wasn't worth fixing. It had to be pulled off the road. I went to drive for another private owner.

The taxi I was driving was old and falling apart. It was going to be pulled off the road in a couple months when the insurance ran out. After about a month, and while I was on shift, I got a phone call that my sister was in an accident in a friend's car and her little one was with her. I raced to the scene of the accident. I was one block away, could see all the emergency vehicles and police, some moron in a jeep blows threw a stop sign and T-boned me on the passenger side. It sent me sliding to the left into oncoming traffic, thankfully there wasn't any. To say the least, the emergency services got there real quick after all. They all thought it was funny, two car accidents, siblings, and a block apart. It was kind of funny.

Well that was the end of my cab driving days, thankfully. The statistics say driving a taxi is the only job that doubles your chances of a heart attack, not even police can say that, at least they are allowed to carry guns to protect themselves. I never drove cab again, no matter how desperate I was for work. It was just way to stressful. The day shift wasn't as bad but it had its moments. It just wasn't for me anymore.

I got unemployment and had to move back in with the family, I couldn't afford the house I was in any more. I moved back into the computer room. After a couple months mom and a couple siblings went to Southern Alberta to visit a brother I had there. My step dad and youngest sister stayed behind with me.

My sisters attitude was incredibly bad, at this time she is about nine or ten years old and did whatever she wanted and never gets punished, it was really getting to me. I was so bored; frustrated that nothing had worked in the last year and a half to get me set up in my own operation. I was up all night, went for walks with Hates at all hours, I was going stir crazy for months.

A couple days after they left, I called mom and told her I was hopping the bus to come to them because I couldn't stay in the house any more, I also needed to get away. I got my unemployment check and got on the next bus headed west. I stayed at my brothers for four or five days and then we headed back. Got a little slack from mom, it was supposed to be her vacation, I didn't care. I was vibrating on the inside for so long and it was getting worse, I had to get out if only for a couple days.

At this point I started to look at life, how could things keep getting so screwed up, everything I tried or touched failed, or was destroyed. I was so disappointed in everything, angry, depressed, and furious with everything, especially at life. It felt like there was a force or something stopping things from coming together. Every time it looked like things were going to get set up, something else came along and destroyed it.

When we got back to BC mom and Bear went to dinner. Not even gone for ten minutes and the youngest was so out of control in her behaviour that I had decided to sell everything I had, buy camping gear and take my dog for a month's long walk. When the folks got back I told them what I was planning, they blew it off like I wasn't serious.

I had a 1984 Ford F-150, short box, four wheel drive. It had the 4.9L inline six cylinder with a five speed manual, ran great but cops pulled it until I could find a box for it. It was rusted over seventy percent threw. I sold it to an auto wreckers for one hundred dollars. I walked down to the pawn shop with my house amp and tuner and traded it for a large back pack. Went to a surplus store, bought a cooler with wheels. If I was going to be walking through the bush I wasn't going to carry it. I bought everything else I needed when my second last unemployment check came in.

Now everyone knew I was serious; it took about a week to throw it all together. I found a milk crate that I was going to strap to the top of the cooler to haul stuff. The plan was to move every day and just walk around the bush for a month. The folks said they were moving out at the end of the month and when I get back the house was mine and we could finally set me up the way I wanted. I didn't really believe it; I thought it was just their way of trying to help relax me.

After talking to a friend of Bears', I had decided to go to a free camp ground that was brought up in conversation. It was better than having to move every day and pack up camp, drag a cooler and try to keep the dog close by. So the next day, I packed up the car and Hatez and off we went. We got there and I was excited, relieved, worried, I felt like a weight was lifting.

I picked the site I wanted, got the car unpacked; the grounds were empty and let the dog loose. The outhouse was just a little ways away and the lake was in the opposite direction about the same distance away. My ride left, just me and the dog. What the hell is that! It is so quite, nothing, the wind, the sound of the lake and the little waves hitting the shore, it was blowing from the lake into my site. Fresh air.

I set up camp. I bought a couple tarps, one went between two tree's, between my tent and the lake. It was there to block the wind for Hatez. One under the tent and a large one over the tent and surrounding area. This way I could keep firewood and other things dry when it rained. I was in a two man tent, it kept my clothes, Hatez and me. Hatez liked to be covered up, even outside, so he had his own blanket.

The first day the grounds were still empty, I pulled out the camping chair and pointed it at the lake. I went back to the tent, inside the side pocket of my back pack was a book, and it was black. I didn't bring a pen, pencil or any paper. I took the book back to my chair and sat down. I took a deep breath, looked out over the lake, looked up at the sky and the trees and said here goes; the first chapter was called Genesis.

After a day or two it was still just me. I was sitting there reading when a dark coloured truck pulled in and down the site to the water, about fifty feet from me. As it passed a voice sounded familiar, then a face popped out from the passenger side window. That looks like; no way what are the odds. I put my bible down and walked toward the water. As I get closer the passenger spots me and pokes his head out, unbelievable, it's a friend of the family's, actually a friend of my first brother but he was around the family so long and everyone liked him. He got out and couldn't believe he found me of all people on top of a mountain, beside a lake with no car. Well the party began. We had some beers and some hoots and sat around the fire. They didn't have any camping gear so they left late and I went to bed with no one around again. It was so peaceful.

On my birthday, I was relaxed and enjoying the day on the side of the lake. I had put my line in the water about twenty minutes earlier and walked back to the site. I could hear this motor boat come running by the shore line. I watched them come down the beach line, I heard one of the three in the boat say, you just hit that guy's line! I looked up in time to watch my rod get pulled into the water, the boat accelerated away. I ran as fast as I could down the road to the point but the boat was gone. I walked back to the site, looked in the water but the rod was gone. I had to use my back up rod, it wasn't a good one but I wasn't catching anything any way.

People started to show up and the grounds had a little life in them, Hatez had to stay on the chain, he didn't like that. I was fishing up and down the side of the lake with little luck. So in the end, I just cast out my rod from the closest point in front of my site. It was the day after my birthday and this new camper was asking if I had heard the news, it was all over the radio and TV for hours worldwide already.

The date was 9/11, I didn't believe it and they were still missing the fourth plane. He had turned on the radio in his truck and we sat there for a couple hours talking about it. That day someone let me use a cell, once we were able to get a signal; I called my mom's and got someone to come get me. They agreed to come get me the next day.

It was about a forty-five minute drive to get to me and then back to town, the road to the site was a rough one. When we got back to town I went straight to the TV. They were just starting dinner so I had to stay for a nice meal too. We got back on the road a little later then I wanted to but I was in such disbelief over what I saw on the TV.

We got lost on the way back and ended up on the other side of the lake. I noticed it when we passed under some power lines and realized the tilt in the road. From the camp site I had looked up here with my binoculars a couple days earlier and knew where we were. I told Bear to stop and turn around, he did and twenty minutes later and we were there. Hatez was curled up under a tree, I had left him behind and it was dark and chilly by the time I got back.

A couple days later, the camp ground still had people in it, someone there had a small boat and they were just coming into the shore. They were about one hundred feet out when one of the woman said "Hey! There is a rod in the water there", as she pointed into the water. They stopped and fished it out. I could hear them and thought what are the odds. I had talked to them earlier, talked to a lot of people while out there and had told them about the boat that took my rod on my birthday. They pulled up to shore and asked if it was mine. It was, that was just too weird.

It rained for at least a week, stuck under that tarp, cooking over a tiny make shift fire, I couldn't make it to big since it was under the tarp. The wind blew from the lake right into my site 80% of the time but it wasn't moving in this weather. I still hadn't caught any fish but macaroni and cheese never tasted so good, hunger is the best sauce. I started reading the bible the day after I got there, on a daily basis. I thought it was odd, 9/11, me on top of a mountain, looking into God. I looked at it in the most logical way I could think of.

If there was a God, a God that created creatures large and small, all vegetation, the stars, moon, planets and then he creates man. If man was meant to live then it only stands to reason that the creator of said life would give the new life a set of rules, guide lines, a list of good and bad things, a list of things that pleased pr displeased him. If man is mortal and said creator wasn't going to show himself for hundreds of years or a couple thousand years at a time, then wouldn't he make sure those rules were handed down correctly? You can take any law or rule and make it say what you want, including the bible's teachings. When a law or rule is passed there is no need to repeat it in future rules and laws. The bible is not a book, it is a mini library. The first four books alone are written over a couple hundred years, but by the same author. The bible repeats itself over and over again, over hundreds of years. The bible and it's origin's are the oldest things written about God. Even if someone tries to change something, the truth still shows threw.

I came to the conclusion, if there is a God then the Old Testament must be true, if so, then the New Testament must be true. I already believed in the devil, so why did I choose to ignore God. You can't have one without the other. Then my life question changed from, "Could I take a life without getting caught and how many times?" The question became, "If I was going to believe in a God, how could I think of taking a life?"

It was a long month and I had lots of time to come to this conclusion. It started to change the way I thought about things a little. I figured I spent so much time reading, studying, planning and put so much fore thought into ending a life, I should put some thought into life. This would take some time apparently. I am still learning more all the time.

I started catching fish about four or five a day before I left the site. It turns out the little bobble that was going on the whole time wasn't weeds, it was fish. I couldn't catch them fast enough, I ate so much fish it wasn't funny. A group of younger people showed up, not kids, early twenties. They caught nothing all day. I had my daily limit and had been eating fish all day. I gave them all I had but one or two and went fishing, caught my limit again. I miss it.

A few days later a camper let me use his phone and I called my mom's to find out when I was getting picked up so I could get to town to get more supplies for the last four or five days. I was told they needed help to move their stuff out and they were coming to get me. I was not impressed. I was looking forward to the last few days. Finally, I was catching fish and my mind was in a much different place. I went fishing; it was still early in the day. Two hours later Bear showed up with a friend of his to pick me up.

That was a lot sooner than expected and hadn't packed up anything, I was just fishing, had caught six or seven by that time. I had to quickly rip down camp, clean the fish and load the car. It took about an hour and a half. We got back to the city and sat on a couch, nice. The house had boxes all over and they were actually moving out.

After waiting almost two years, I finally have a different outlook on life and what it means and now I am getting set up into a grow operation. I was slightly conflicted with where my head was and what I was about to get involved with. They moved out and I suddenly had my own place, oh so quite.

They moved into this huge house with a double car garage. The garage had been converted to a grow room. While I was at the lake the house I was moving into had the basement converted but it was a tiny room and suddenly there was a third partner I didn't know about. My share in that house just paid my share of the bills so I never seen any cash, I went back to work doing deliveries.

In their house, the room was big enough for about fifteen to eighteen plants, taller than me and at least feet feet in diameter. It was a site to see. I had kind of been thinking about stuff from the lake but was still conflicted; I spent the next year or so playing an online game with Bear. There were two computers in their house so after work I would go by and level up my character with Bear all night.

After a year or so I was getting tired of playing that stupid game and had done a lot of thinking about life and what it was about. I started to do some research online; I did this for a few months. I came across so much information, I printed off a fraction of it and still have it all, but I have never shown anyone, not even Subject X.

I ended up having to move out of the house I was in, the third partner screwed everything up and another couple took it over because it wasn't paying for itself. Hatez and I ended up moving back in with the family in the big house. The cost of living was just too high to get a place with my dog.

My youngest brother, we will call him Younger, had just turned seventeen and was living in Southern Alberta with our father. He was being beaten almost every day and needed to get out. He was young and careless, mom and Bear couldn't do it with what they had going on. I agreed to take custody of him and he moved to Vernon, with me at moms. The condition was to get on social assistance and get our own place. It didn't take long but Younger got us kicked out of moms within a month. If he had to go, so did I because I was his legal guardian.

He was already having problems in the city with people so I made the decision to move him out of town about twenty-five kilometres to a small town. A friend had some room at his place; he was renting the basement from his mother. He had two large dogs, two komodo dragons, a tarantula and a scorpion. He also shared a room with a female friend of his, not dating, just friends with benefits.

Again it took under two months to get evicted because of the total lack of respect from my brother. He would open the basement door and let Hatez out without a chain, the older lady would be in the garden and my dog scared her several times this way. The lady would make homemade bread every day, Younger, would always go for the fresh stuff and leave a mess. When she was on the phone a few times, his friends would pick up the other line and scream obscenities in to it. She was retired and didn't need the stress, my friend asked me to find our own place.

I found the main floor of a house and rented it. It was a three bedroom, non smoking place only a couple blocks from my friends. I was driving a 1980 AMC eagle, four wheel drive, hatchback and installed two sets of head lamps on the front. I took Hatez into town for a visit at my mom's. I let him out for a pee and he bolted off, it was a huge yard, couple acres. I could hear some kind of scuffle in the bush, I called him but nothing. My sixth sense kicked in and I knew something was seriously wrong. I ran into the house grabbed my shoes and car keys.

I got into the car and turned on all eight head lamps and lit up the front of the garage. I put it in reverse and hammered it backwards, got the car pointed in the direction of the noise, put it in to drive and stepped on it. I got to the barb wire fence, stopped and got out. As I walked to the front of the car I could see Hatez walking towards me, then another set of eyes came up behind him and bit him in the butt. He spun around and the eye's disappeared, Hatez turned around and started walking towards me again, all of a sudden I could see at least half a dozen sets of eye's coming up behind him. OH wow, this was a new one. I went to the fence and made some noise; Hatez came under the fence and got in the car. When I got him in the house, I found bite marks all over his back side and a huge gash in his right side closer to the top. It was almost three inches long, one inch wide and at least a quarter inch deep. I called my friend out where I was living. He had a friend that was a vet and got me a cone and some sort of medicine that needs to be applied and bandaged.

I was doing deliveries to make ends meet and had to drive back and forth for work. I came home early one night and all the lights were on, TV and play station were on, my brother was gone. Damn! The dog was on the couch with no cone and was licking and gnawing at his wounds, I was instantly pissed. The wound was now bigger then when it happened, I put the cone on him and called my buddy to see if Younger was there, he was, I told him to get home. He blew it off like nothing. I wanted to smack the crap out of him but didn't lay a hand on him.

We smoked in the back bedroom with the window open, door closed and blew the smoke out the window. Late at night once in a while, I would smoke in the living room but I opened the windows or patio, no matter how cold it was. I came home another night after work Younger and my buddy were sitting there smoking and toking and the house was full of smoke. Younger said he wasn't expecting me back so early, I asked my friend to leave and I tried to talk to Younger but it was useless.

Again I was at work, my brother called and said he was stuck at the corner store with Hatez and some kids out front were giving him grief. One of them had gotten off his bike, picked it up and threw it at my brother and dog. I booked off work and hammered it home. I got about ten minutes out of town and he called back and was at home with Hatez. I turned around and went back to work. I found out a few days later he had been intimating people with my dog; he was causing his own problems.

His schooling went downhill and he figured he could do whatever he wanted. Smoke when and where he wanted, he moved back with my buddy, which pissed my off. If he is not with me, I get kicked off assistance and have to move, again. We met at his school with a teacher. The three of us were standing in the parking lot and right off the start he said he wasn't coming back and screw me, he was almost an adult and my rules were unfair, he walked away.

This all happened in about three months. I had to move back to town with my family. In the end Younger went back to Southern Alberta. I was still doing deliveries trying to deal with the continual pile of crap I called a life. Due to a stupid move, we had to pack up and leave BC as soon as possible, we had heat bagged ourselves out in a bad way. It had been two years, time to move. We all packed up and moved to Southern Alberta. I was now thirty years old.

CHAPTER 7

'SOUTHERN ALBERTA'

Before we got here, yes I still live here in southern Alberta seven years later, there was a friend of Bear's who said he had a tent trailer that I could buy and move into when we got here so I wasn't staying with family again, he made a deal with Bear and I owed him one thousand dollars for it, it sounded nice. He also had a 1989 Plymouth Sundance I could take on with pay you later agreement for eight hundred dollars.

I drove the AMC Eagle from BC and had gone through over eight litres of oil, in a construction zone one of the flag girls waved to me and said I was leaking antifreeze all over, I yelled back, "It's not antifreeze, it's oil!" It made it and ran great outside of stopping every couple hours for oil.

When we got everything to Southern Alberta we went to set up this tent trailer. I got to buddies place and as he was trying to set it up, a pole snapped. It was a very old unit, never seen one before or since. It was literally a tent mounted to a trailer, old school. It was mouldy inside and the instant I saw it I knew there was no way I was living in it. I could see the frustration on Bear's face, he didn't want me to move in again and I didn't want to, but ultimately I had no choice. Hatez of course was with me.

I went for the first job I knew I could get deliveries. I was going through so much oil in my car; I really needed that Sundance in my possession. Finally I got it, insured and registered, it went through more gas then my AMC did. I put it in the shop and they said the motor was blown and was lucky it still drove. I was furious. I still couldn't catch a break to get something going. I went to the guy we got the car from, Bear's friend, I got there about quarter to ten at night, I remember that clearly. I knocked on the door nicely; I was fuming but knew I couldn't go nuts because he was a childhood friend of Bear's.

He told us his mechanic said it was good, reliable and a good deal. I asked what exactly his mechanic said, because I got paper work here that says it is garbage. He got all defensive with me and I got angry back. I went straight home, I was so pissed off. Mom could see that and asked what was wrong, I explained what happened, she understood. We had noticed the time for some reason; it wasn't even quarter after ten yet.

I left, I don't remember where to or for how long but when I got back mom said it was a good thing I left. The guy had called Bear and told him that I was pounding on the door after ten o'clock, his kids were sleeping and I was yelling at him from the start. Apparently Bear wanted to beat the crap out of me. Mom had talked to him and got it through to him that it wasn't me, I was home and talking to mom by ten and it wasn't like me just to show up at someone's house and start yelling. He calmed done after a bit and went to bed. Everything was fine the next morning. We ended up giving the car back to him at a loss, no choice it was useless.

I bought a little blue car and just started working for a delivery service. After a month or so things were very stressful at home. We were all cramped into this little house, with my dog. Bear had made himself two peanut butter and jam sandwiches; he left them on the washing machine as he entered the bathroom. The stairs to go up to the computer rooms were right there, when he came out his sandwiches were gone.

He got right pissed off and told me the dog had to go. He was too much of a pain to keep around anymore. Now I was pissed, over a couple sandwiches? He knew not to leave food laying around. I called lots of kennels but because he was a pit bull and I had no papers on him, no one would take him. I finally talked to a very nice lady who told me to come by so we could talk. She was hesitant but agreed to do it. It was three hundred dollars a month plus food, I brought the food because he got the good stuff. He was in there locked up for two months. She had a dugout there so I went out every two or three days at least to visit and exercise him.

After that I made arrangements to move into the bosses' garage he had in the industrial area. It was just a regular dirty garage that had an upstairs but I was allowed to get my dog back so I moved in. It was dirty and cramped, there was no way to clean it, and so I kept sandals by the bed. Every time I wanted to get up I had to put them on, or my shoes.

I was only supposed to be the night driver but the first Saturday, I was there he showed up at eleven in the morning and asked why I wasn't answering my phone. I worked until three in the morning the night before. He owned hotdog carts that sit in front of the bars, they didn't get cleaned until five that morning, I was tired. I got up and started work, from then on while working there I had to work whenever he needed me.

One of the restaurant owners and I became friends, we will call him Sneaky, he had told me about this trailer his wife and him had for rent in a trailer park. They said that I could rent it and all I had to do was register with the head office so they knew how many people were in the dwelling, I paid the rent and planned the move for the end of the month.

I told my boss I was moving out, I didn't want to quit until after I was moved out and had another job. The landlord helped take over the first load; we dropped off the dog and the AMC and went back for more. Well it turns out it was an application to get into the trailer park, not a registration. While we went for the next load the park manager showed up to find out what was going on and when he got to the door my dog made a real fuss. He said the whole trailer wall moved when the dog came at the window and it wasn't allowed in the park.

After a couple of days of fighting with him, the landlord said I had to get out or they would have to move the trailer out of the park. So back to the garage I went. The landlord said they had this little house for rent at end of month, four hundred dollars a month, mine if I wanted, I wanted! A house for that price and no issues with my dog, I jumped on it. I was there for five years, until they illegally evicted me, that is another story.

While in this house, I had quit working for the delivery service and went to work for a pizza place, good money but they were so busy it could get rather stressful. After a bit I had to quit and go work for a higher class place doing deliveries. Best delivery job I have ever had, Been doing business with this company for over six years, I still work there at the present time.

I had quit after about a year and started a delivery service. I saw a need and demand and tried to fill it. Operating this company put me to an edge I never thought possible. I owned it for two and a half years and worked over one hundred hours a week. After the first year, I was just coming out of a relationship with, let's call her the Gambler and she really did a number on me. I was so out of control, if my drivers had any problem with a customer I would show up and yell and scream at the client. I was very strict with restaurants; my road rage took on a life of its own.

My driving was well beyond bad, I probably should have had my license taken away a few times. My favourite move with my cars has always been the same. As a delivery driver you need a small car, most small cars are front wheel drive with the emergency brake between the front seats. If there was someone following to close, or I wanted to piss someone off, this is how I did it and it worked every time.

All of the following steps must be done at the same time, 1—put your left foot over the brakes so the lights come on but no pressure to decrease speed, 2-pull emergency brake so the rear tires lock up and start to smoke, 3—hit the gas to accelerate away. The car behind you thinks you are stopping and hammers on their brakes, meanwhile you are accelerating away. That was the ultimate way to get to someone and like I said, it worked every time.

I have dozens of stories, I have been knocked out on a side street in Vernon by a stranger because I was arguing with an old man for cutting me off, I have been convicted of a couple road rage incidents, had to chase people, been chased, never caught though. If there is anything I am really good at, it is driving, I can do things that make people wonder how the hell I could have learned that. I can pull a car into a 180 degree spin and end up parked on the other side of the street.

Two years ago my insurance agency told me in the previous two years I had insured twenty two different cars. Two of those were for others but the rest were mine. I wrecked cars all the time, slammed into curbs; tree's or just killed it from being so hard on it. I did a count about a year ago, in my life I have owned about sixty cars, only about four were parts cars, the rest I drove for one week to one year. I always had a backup car or two insured for a while, I needed job security. As a delivery driver you need back up cars to keep your job, at least I did.

When the relationship ended with Gambler, I decided to sell the company and do anything else. It took a year to sell and ended up giving it away just to get away from it on January 1/07. In order to make it a done deal, I had to sublet the house. I sold it to a mechanic friend of mine. I bought a motor home and moved it into the driveway. I was still on the property, just not in the house. I was there till the end of October 2008.

Since October 2008 I have been renting the basement at my mom's house. I moved out for about four months but it didn't last. I have had the opportunity to move out since but if I had, my mom wouldn't have been able to keep the house and have to move herself. She is running a business out of here, she couldn't afford a move. It was also cheap rent so it gave me a chance to put something together. I always wanted to do something different from everyone else.

Here I am in June of 2011 and I have finally got a business that has a real possibility of being a success. Regular hours and a good income. I have plans to start an online company that will make online anything safer, yep this system has a wide range of applications and will make the internet a safer place.

Chapter 8

'Past Betrayals'

I had a girlfriend sleep with my roommate when I was twenty and living in Lethbridge, because I wouldn't leave the party I was hoisting to go home with her. Funny thing, the next day when she told me, she asked me to hit her so that we would be even and could move past it, I couldn't do it and walked away instantly. A couple weeks later she came by the house to try to get with the roommate again, he wanted nothing to do with her.

While I owned the taxi back in Saskatchewan, I helped Gij get his license so he could come and work for me. He had passed his security test through the police so I paid to have him go through a course to get his taxi license. Then suddenly after he got it, he said he didn't want to drive, we weren't very good friends after that. The company started to give me grief at this point for not being able to find a day driver.

About two months before I had lost my first taxi there was an owners meeting. The taxi company had hired a new dispatcher, we will call her Around, she was young, blonde and had blue eyes. She had a real attitude on the radio with the driver's, except me. The meeting was all about her and she had to be fired. I was standing at the door with my financial backer and one of the drivers said maybe all the driver's don't want to fire her! Maybe a driver is dating her! He finished his sentence in my face.

My backer looked at him and said so what! We had started dating a couple weeks earlier. That night we were watching a movie and the phone rang. I was living in a hotel room, a kitchenette. On the phone was one of the other car owners, he said he understood my position but Around was fired, I said I understood. He asked if I was going to tell her or if he should tell her on the phone. I said no problem I would do it. I hung up and crawled back into bed. I told her I had some bad news, she just got fired from dispatching. She blew it off, it was a crumby job she said.

We broke up, I forget why. As a taxi driver I had come across her leaving the bar, she saw me and just had to jump in with her friends, she was letting some guy bring her home, and she did that a few times just to get to me. She called me one night; she was partying just a couple doors down in another room and wanted to talk. I said ok and she came to my room. We talked and ended up back together.

With me working nights she was able to party all night with whoever she wants until whenever, I didn't get off work until at least five in the morning. It turns out she had started to see Gij while I was at work, which is what my suspicion was anyway. Well within a couple weeks it was thrown in my face. We were at my place one night and the phone rang, it was Gij, asking to speak to her. I handed her the phone, guess I had my proof. She hung up and we went to bed, I believe I broke it off the next day.

About two months after I came back from the top of the mountain in BC and took over the house, I met a woman. It was a Friday evening; I had just walked out of my house and turned left on the sidewalk. I had taken a couple of steps and saw this woman standing on the corner. My sixth sense clicked when I saw her, something about the look on her face. I was just going for a walk around and as I was passing by her, she said, "Can you help me?" I stopped dead in my tracks, looked at the ground. My subconscious said "No! Keep Moving!" and my head started to shake no but it was someone asking for help, I had to stop. I asked her what the problem was. She said she had no place to go. I had this house with four bedrooms and was only using one, so why not.

We went the thirty feet to my place and went in. We sat and talked and I learned that she had been in a car accident many years ago and was thrown through a windshield and she was in a coma for a little while. We will call her Spaced. Her mom and her were very close and shortly after, her mom had killed herself. She had come out of the coma on the day her mother killed herself, it messed her up but so did the windshield.

She got a large settlement, couple million but had a trustee that paid for everything. She owned the house but the trustee had care of it. She felt trapped, controlled and bored; she had a live in care giver also. It all seemed a little odd, she didn't seem unbalanced and our conversations were mutual and coherent. I didn't watch TV and the radio in the car didn't work. She spent the weekend and we started seeing each other.

I was telling her all weekend to call in and let them know she was ok, she never did. Monday she finally called them and said she was coming to get some clothes. We got in the car and headed up to her place. We got there and there was this guy, the caregiver that was at the house, he told her, he had called the cops. It seemed like a little overkill to me at the time. She packed some stuff; we got in the car and headed out, turned a corner and here comes a cop with lights and sirens and immediately stopped me and demanded that she get out of the car.

I was stunned. It turned out she had been reported missing on Friday and was all over the TV and radio. The officer was rude yelling didn't I watch TV or listen to the radio! I said no but she didn't believe me. The officer demanded that Spaced get out of the car, I had to talk her out and she got out and I told her to call me when she needed a ride. She got in with the cop and left.

I didn't realize what her situation was but she was apparently brain damaged from the accident and that was putting it mildly. We will leave it at that. She had met some other friends and the one; we will call him Kaz, kept talking to her about how big he was down below. This went on for a couple weeks before she told me because she knew it would bother me.

We had an argument one night and I went home, I told her I would call her the next day. The next day, I called her and she was stunned, she thought we were done, I said I would call and did. We agreed to go for a drive, I got to her house and Kaz was coming down the stairs tucking in his shirt, he walked past me and out the door. I saw that look in her eyes; I have seen that look to many times. I ignored it. We stayed together for a bit after but she was spending too much time with Kaz and I was done. And she ended up with someone else within a week.

I was with the entrepreneur; she had two kids, one boy about four and a girl about a year younger. I had just moved to Southern Alberta and was doing deliveries for a pizza place in town where she worked. After a month or so there were not enough deliveries for me to make a living so I had to quit and go work for another delivery service. I swung into the pizza place once in a while and me and the entrepreneur hit it off.

We started dating and I enjoyed spending time with her and her kids. After about six months or so she had the opportunity to buy the restaurant she was working at. She got some financing and pulled it off with bringing in a partner, I forget his name. He was taking money out of the till and gambling it away. She got rid of him after a while and hired a friend of hers to manage the till. Then he needed a place to live and she let him move in. We were never alone, he was always there and I always got the sense that something happened between them, something non sexual but romantic.

I found out a couple months later that he had written her a lengthy love letter; it wasn't very nice towards me. That is why he never left us alone, he was doing it to cause a wedge, if he is up late, others would stay and visit him. I am sure that we broke up because we were never alone. With her business, two kids, the friend and all the others that never left us alone, I couldn't take it anymore and broke it off. It turns out that she became an alcoholic behind my back. She bought at least two bottles a day from the liquor store next door and mixed it with her coffee. I don't drink coffee, so no worries about me stealing a sip.

I cared for her kids and wasn't allowed to see them anymore. I was crushed, and vowed never to get involved like that again, the pain is too much. I kept in touch with the grandmother for a while to hear about the kids, or at least that is what I told myself. It has been over six years and I still visit the grandmother once in a while.

I was single for about four months when I met the Gambler. She was bipolar and had a ten year old daughter. I had no idea what that meant and didn't care, she was sexy. When the relationship started, I was running my second delivery service, this time in Southern Alberta. I had hired her as a driver but it took under a week for us to start hanging out. The first night she stayed, we didn't have sex; I had bought a 6 pack of beer. She said one or two should not mess with her medication, it didn't even take one. She ended up getting sick for a couple hours and then we went to bed to sleep it off. If you're on medication that strong, you need to follow the directions but alcohol turned out to be only one vice this poor woman had. She was into some hard drugs but it was the gambling that killed me.

She was by far the luckiest person I have ever seen on those machines, VLT's. She won all the time and was able to max the machines at twenty-five hundred dollars many times. With me running a delivery service I had very little real time to devote to a relationship. I was devoted to the business.

My father passed away around this time, I had not talked to him in at least twelve years. I did not go to the funeral, it was in a church. I showed up at the end and stayed outside the room it was held in. Gambler said I might regret it one day but I doubt it, he made his choices, I made mine. I saw him about a year earlier. I was driving by my brother's place and saw him working on his truck with some other people. I stopped in to say hi, as I was walking passed the back of the truck; dad had turned around and looked at me. I recognized him immediately, turned around and walked away never to see him again.

Gambler went to rehab here in the area for her gambling. In order to do it, her twelve year old daughter had to go to her parents and she moved her whole house into my tiny one bedroom house. We stored her car in the back yard; it was only for three weeks. I brought her smokes and loonies for the pop machine every day and was there for her graduation at seven in the morning. I worked all night doing deliveries but still made it.

Things were good for about a week and then bang, a whole new and addicted woman appeared. She was suddenly jealous, angry and almost violent, disappearing all the time. I was working so much I didn't have the patience or the time to try to help her. I did spend hours driving around looking for her at places that had VLT's. Things went downhill fast.

She was working at a pizza place; I had just fired her for stealing from a liquor store. She told them she didn't have a float and would be right back with the money. Everyone knew she was with me, they knew I would cover it. When I pulled up out back and she came out, she was very hostile. I owned the delivery service and did business with this pizza place. She got right in my face, was bouncing me with her chest, her hands. She was trying to provoke me into hitting her, never even came close, I just can't hit a woman. In the end after a couple days we talked it out. We got back together but she stayed working at the pizza place.

We broke up again; she did it to the pizza place she was working at. I was able to track her down; she won some money and gave me the money back. She went to work directly for another contract of mine. They were a busy restaurant and one night she took around three hundred dollars of their money. She disappeared and they called me. I had made it clear to all my contracts from the beginning not to hire my drivers from me, they did anyway and with some sweet talking on her part, I am sure. When they called and I said I had fired her and wasn't responsible for what happened, they got really agree, changed to another company and told everyone they knew my drivers would steal their money. Business owners always know other business owners. It was just before Christmas when it happened the last time. I was so angry and what not, I had found out she was on social assistance while working the last couple months, so I called the fraud department and reported her just before Christmas, they said they would get to it in the new year.

She had kept the charger and hand held radio that we used for communication for the business. She wouldn't call me back about getting the radio and charger back from her. Before I called the fraud department I ended up learning that if she used the radio, whether to talk, interrupt dispatch or steal deliveries, she would be in massive trouble. It turns out that the airways are monitored by the federal government also. It is up to one hundred and fifty thousand dollars in finds and ten years in prison for using a hand held radio on a repeater without authorization. I had already talked to whom I needed and as soon as she used the radio in any manner they were going to send down a truck to track her. They are not like the police, they do not need a warrant, and suspicion is enough. I figured she could use the time in lock up, it would help her get sober, I was way to revengeful back then.

When I finally did get hold of her, she said she had dropped it off and I needed to find it. I called the police and had an officer go over there, it was better than me going over there. She let him search the house and he did not find anything. After the officer left, he came to my place and said he didn't find it. She called later and said she had hung it on a fence post in the backyard two days earlier, in the middle of January. Found it.

She showed up New Years Eve in a red dress, high heels and two wine glasses in her hand. One was a tinted yellow and the other was tinted blue. She wanted to celebrate it with me. The instant I saw her standing there, I knew I had screwed up; I knew I had crossed a line with that phone call. I invited her in and didn't tell her. I was sure if I had; she would have left then and there and gone done some hard drugs. We spent the night together and the next morning I felt worse but still couldn't, didn't have the nerve is more like it, to tell her. I tried to figure a way out of it for a couple days but then she showed up freaking out and it was all over. I felt so bad I just sat there and let her get it all out and then she left.

At the time I was working over 100 hrs a week and had been doing so for over 1 year. I owned the delivery service, was a control freak and my road rage was ridiculous, I let my anger control me. Once things ended in the New Year, she started dating someone within a week; I went off the deep end. Through the hospital here in town there is a mental emergency unit that is in a residential area that allows people to stay there for a couple days. They offer counselling and help connect you with agencies and contacts all over town that help people going through a rough time. I parked my car at home, handed over the whole company over to my family for two days and checked myself in. There was a curfew at ten in the evening, after working one hundred hour a week for almost a year and a half, it was tough to sleep. I and tossed and turned those nights. I had to stop driving for a couple days because she lived on one of the main drags, doing deliveries I passed her place all day and night and I knew what the candle in the bedroom window meant.

I also went for a bunch of blood test's to see if there was something wrong. I was hoping something would explain why my thought process was the way it was. After the tests came in, they said I had HEP-C. I had gone through tests back in Saskatchewan but was under the impression that I was cleared. They are sure this time. I have to go talk to my last two girl friends, not this again. So I did, I made contact and informed them. They both got tested, they both were cleared. What a relief.

I know I was burnt out and tired of life but the biggest reason I had to take a break was the betrayal of her. Is that fair? I did call her in. And all though I feel bad for that call, a bigger part of me thinks she deserved it and worse. Again, is that just the anger? That was over five years ago. Unfortunately there is much more to it. I was so frustrated and hurt that she was already with someone else; I drove by many times in the alley to memorize his van and plate number. Small little details so I could pick it out of a crowd from a distance. Believe it or not, it's a good thing I familiarized myself with it.

Not even one month later I spotted the van scoping out my house. I drove an Acura Integra with a fuel pump issue. I was headed home at about one in the morning and saw the van just driving in front of my house, four blocks in front of me. I could not give away it was me so made the next right and stepped on it. I went around the block and made a total of three quick rights, when I was approaching the corner to see down the street in front of the house, I killed the lights and crept up. When I got to the corner I turned off the ignition and waited. Sure enough it pulled up in front of the house and the passenger door and sliding door opened and two people jumped out.

I grabbed the phone and called the police. I told them I was watching someone break into my house; they told me they were too busy to spare anyone. So I tried to start my car, damn fuel pump, wouldn't start. They came out, jumped into the van and took off. My car still wouldn't start. It took me about two minutes to finally get it started.

I raced home and found my side door ajar, I walked in and noticed some change containers missing. They took two tobacco containers of dimes, nickels and quarters. And Hates was sitting on the couch all curled up. I was on the phone with the cops as I walked out the door, still too busy, call back in a bit. I got in the car and headed toward her house, got there, no van. I drove around for couple hours, still going by her place to check. Finally!! The van is there, cops still too busy but asks a few more questions. Turns out because of where I was parked and the fact that the side door was on the opposite side of the house, I didn't see them actually enter the house. This means they would do nothing.

That was my last straw. The next day I bought a wireless camera and monitor security system. The bathroom door was right behind the side door to the house, so on the inside of the bathroom, above the door, I hung a pump action pellet gun. Behind the house door I put a steel pole about three and a half feet long. I believe I had a knife or two around the area on the desk. As soon as you open the back door to go outside, there were concrete stairs, three and then the driveway. Beside the porch to the right was the BBQ. I took the camera, put it into a small box with a hole in the side, wrapped it in a cloth to stop it from rolling around inside and put it in the BBQ. The lid rested on top of the box to hold it still. The desk was across from the bathroom door, the house door opened between them. I had two TV's, one for farmer vision, one for the camera and VCR.

I sat there many a nights just waiting for it, sure enough. I had all the lights off, so I cracked the door to look, ya it was them again. I grabbed the gun and pole and went into the yard. My yard was dark so it was easy to hide and watch. That's when I added the sling shot. They must have gotten spooked because they didn't come back. I sat there for a another couple months waiting, I even parked my car a block or two away to make it look like I wasn't home a couple times. They did come by at least two dozen times, I was always ready for them but they never stopped again, probably a good thing, I might not be big but the element of surprise and a couple weapons go a long way.

One afternoon some friends were helping me work on one of my many cars and the van drove passed, it was broad daylight. It parked up the block in front of another vehicle. We all stood there and watched them. I wasn't paying attention but a blonde walked by, but by the time I noticed her she was too far away with her back for me to identify. She did walk to the van and get in. As she was walking to it, we were discussing running up there and confronting them but they left as we were talking about it.

After a couple months, I went online to meet some woman. I met this wonderfully neurotic clean freak. Sorry dear but you are awfully neat. She was a wonderful woman, we will call her Neat, but it only lasted for about a couple weeks, then we stayed friends or tried. We met on fathers' day and I was taking Hatez to the lake. We spent a couple hours out there, came back to my place and had a BBQ, then sat outside and had some drinks.

After it got late around midnight, a friend had stopped by. She was someone I had slept with about two weeks earlier. She walked up to the house saying she was here to spend the night and she was going to bed, she walked into the house and got into bed. I was a little stunned to tell you the truth. You could see the unsure surprise expression on my date's face, as I think she saw mine.

It was everything my friends could do not to bust a gut laughing at me. Then she comes to the back door, opens it and she is only wearing a t-shirt. I forget what we all talked about; I was trying to figure out how the hell this happened. She closed the door and went to bed. We sat around and had a couple more drinks and my date left with this kind of, what the hell kind sort of look, I couldn't blame her; I was still working on it myself.

After everyone left, I went to bed. We didn't have sex that night, although I did try. I felt guilty for a while for that but not half as much for what was to come. My date from that night and I hung out for the next week or so and we tried to have sex but I was still so angry from the previous relationship, my performance sucked and I was in no condition to be involved in a relationship. About ten more days and we hadn't tried it again. One night we were sitting around and you could cut the tension with a knife. The phone rings, I answered it, it was Gambler. She was at a restaurant in town and needed to talk, she was crying. At first I was speechless; my first thought was it was a set up. So I left my Neat at my place, and because she was afraid of dogs I took Hatez.

When I got to the restaurant she was inside, she started to walk toward me and one of the owners gave me a 'WOW' look when we were walking out. This was a restaurant I did business with and the first one she took money from. We went into the parking lot. She asked for help and I said something like how can I help? What do you want from me? The talk lasted about a minute before she walked down the street crying, it broke my heart but she was in a bad place and being unreasonable. I went back home, told my Neat the bad news. I told her I just didn't have it in me to get involved with anyone and I still was torn up over the Gambler. She said she could see it and friends would be fine. I can tell when someone is holding back and felt bad for dragging her into my life and drama. We stayed friends for two or three years after but that has since ended. She was very disappointed to learn about Subject X and me being together almost two years later. We stayed friends for a while but it was hard on her, she did a lot to help me with business cards and stuff over those years and the one time she asked for my help, I couldn't. She had to move a ton of boxes and my back was sore and I could not afford to take the risk of pulling it and being down for work. Since then we haven't talked. That was about four months ago.

However the night I met Gambler at the restaurant, is not over. Once I got back from meeting her and talked to Neat, she left and I sat there and thought about everything. Around one in the morning I got another call from Gambler, she was at another restaurant and had racked up a twenty dollar bill and they were going to call the cops on her. As I walked out the door I thought how funny it was I was going to bail her out so she didn't get arrested, when I was trying so hard to get her arrested a few months earlier.

I got to the restaurant and I believe there were two waitresses watching her so she didn't leave. I paid the bill and we walked out, she had her head down. I had no idea what to do; we got in the car and headed to my place. I told her she could stay on my love seat in the office. I was going out of my head about what to do. Once we got to the office, my house, I rolled a joint and went outside and paced hard core as I smoked it.

I wanted so badly to hold her that night but I knew that wasn't a good idea. Her boyfriend was at her place, they got into a fight and she left. In the end, I told her what I had learned about the counselling house through the hospital. I told her in the morning I would let her make the call then drop her off at hospital. The next morning she did and then we got into the car. Once we got to the hospital and we got out saying our farewells, she asked me for a hug, at first I declined but I am sure I did in the end. That was a hard thing to do. Unfortunately it didn't help her, within a week the van was back in my neighbourhood, it could have just been him looking to see if she was at my place, she wasn't and hasn't been since.

When I had to sit down with Neat tell her that I wasn't ready to date anyone, I could see how hurt she was. I told her about the night before and dealing with my ex and dropping her off at the hospital that morning. I told her she spent the night, on the love seat and after dealing with that I needed to be single for a while.

The gambler and I have talked a few times since. We worked together two years ago at a plant building trailers. We met at the court house a few times and sat, had a smoke and talked. Funny, it was usually when Subject X and I were on the outs. Gambler seems to be doing good now; I ran into her a couple weeks ago again, I wish her all the best.

CHAPTER 9

'SUBJECT X PART 1'

At this time, I was still having issues with Gambler scoping out my house, I met Subject X within a week of meeting Neat on father's day. When I met Subject X, I was pissed at woman and wouldn't even consider having another girlfriend with kids, or even wanted kids. I had just met Neat and was having issues there so I wasn't looking to meet any one else when I met her, just trying to expand my friendship ring, I had few friends. I didn't break up with Neat to go out with Subject X, which was almost one year later; it just worked out that way. I was rude, crude and pushed the envelope just to piss women off, it didn't matter who they were, outside of family, and even that is debatable. I was civil and polite with Neat but it was hard to keep my mouth shut. I hated them all; they were only good for one thing, again debatable. They were all cheating, self-righteous, hypocritical, two faced, back stabbing, conniving, liars. It took a lot to change that, actually it took falling in love with the wrong one to realize each is different.

I had been running my second delivery service for just over a year when I had hired a guy that turned into a good friend; we will call him the Mechanic. He was a few years older than me, short blond hair, glasses and rather thin. He came along just after Gambler and I split up. Over the period of a couple months, he had told me of this female friend he had. He said we would be great friends because we could each dish out the attitude and each of us had a great sense of humour. We had talked a few times on the phone in the week before we met. Something about her voice was so darn attractive.

I met Subject X about a week after fathers' day, that father's day I was having drinks with Neat, some friends and then had that other girl crawl into my bed. The day I met Subject X at her place it was the middle of the afternoon, she was in the spare bedroom off the kitchen, which was also the hang out and smoking room. She had long blond hair, blue eyes and a shinning smile. She was wearing this pink with black trim PJ shirt, it was basically hanging off of her, and you could see her breasts when she moved to fast or leaned forward. She was sitting on the couch with some friends, when we looked at each other and our eye's met for the first time and she smiled and looked so full of life, it was summer time, not even a week into July 2006, I knew I could marry this one, something about her eye's and smile was so intriguing.

It was December of 2005 when I decided it was time to get rid of the company and starting the new year, I started to look for a buyer. Working over one hundred hours a week had really taken a toll on me after a year and a half. In the end I could not find a buyer and sold it to Mechanic January 01/2007 for one dollar. I needed to get rid of it at any cost, before it killed me, or I blacked out and went too far.

Subject X and I hung out a lot during the friendship phase which lasted until her birthday the following May. During this time I fell hard for her. I was working seven days a week and she was never home before two in the morning, well maybe once a week. She spent all her time with, let's call them D and T. This was an alright couple; he was dark haired, a few pounds heavier then me and played the guitar. She had long dark hair, about the same build as Subject X. She was there all night getting high and visiting. I spent a lot of time during that period sitting around waiting for her. Between deliveries I would go by to visit and waited for hours for her to come home. Her house was always a mess because her daughters never cleaned up after themselves or was made to. The dishes got done maybe three times a week and all her home time was spent in the spare room watching TV, until she got on the computer. The time we did spend together talking and hanging out was great. It was nice to have a friend like that, she was my best friend in a long time, if not ever. Some people thought we were together months before we actually were, that's how good we were around each other. We talked about what we wanted in life, how we wanted to live, where we wanted to live, everything and we weren't even together, or sleeping together. Just friends, it was truly amazing.

Everyone could see there was some major connection between us. We connected on every level so well it was amazing, I never had that before. However I saw that her life style and mine would clash, hard. Then her birthday came around and she wanted a kiss, her boyfriend was back at home up North. I kissed her like I have never kissed anyone, it was so sensual and passionate, and it was awesome. Unfortunately, it put me in a position that really concerned me. Outside of her not breaking up with her boyfriend first, I have a medical issue that I would have to bring up. She had this massive smile and bewildered look on her face, she said 'WOW, best birthday kiss she ever had, let alone the best kiss she ever had.' She actually has brought that kiss up several times over the last four years. She wanted to break it off with her boyfriend before we went any further, to me that and showed real character on her part, as far as I was concerned and I agreed. After about two weeks we finally spent the night together, she still hadn't called her boyfriend, she called him two days later. I was there when she called him, she beat around the bush with him but she did eventually say it was over between them.

After my experiences from ages sixteen to twenty three with woman over that STD I never even had, I was very hesitant about hooking up with Subject X because I didn't want to deal with the rejection from telling her. After such a short time we were such good friends, within one month of meeting we were connecting. I didn't want to show her the two pages I had printed off on the subject out of fear of not only rejection but humiliation. I really liked her, I never felt so strong about someone so fast and I wasn't sure if this would screw it all up. I had already made a connection with the children and didn't want Subject X to freak about my issue and keep me from the kids either. I had no other place to hang out but over there, or home and wasn't sure of her reaction, especially since she had kids. I liked her too much and wanted to be with her so after a couple days of hard thinking, I told her.

In the two weeks before we hooked up, we had talked about my health issue, I had given her the two pages I printed off, this way she could take her time and do some research of her own. She took a couple of days and said it was not an issue and we started seeing each other shortly after. We talked about it many times over the next few years about getting healthier. We were able to talk about anything and everything, our dreams, aspirations, wants, needs, desires, everything. Around this time I stopped visiting the grandmother of Entrepreneur to respect the woman I was with. She said she loved the fact that even after all that time; I was still concerned and curious about Entrepreneur's kids. She said it was one of the reason's she wanted to be with me and would never hold Spunky from me no matter what happened.

We hid the first year from everyone, or at least we tried too. I was still hanging around Neat, I didn't want her to feel hurt, it didn't work in the end. Subject X said her brother gets rude and aggressive to her boyfriends; he was living in the house with Mechanic where the motor home I was living in was parked. She and her ex-boyfriend were still friends and he came to visit her from up North many times, he even spent the night at her house a couple times, on the couch. She didn't want him to be hurt. Everyone could see it anyways. We had so much fun with it, she would sit on my lap when no one was around, steel a kiss when she could, I grabbed her ass every chance I could, I loved watching that woman smile and see those eyes twinkle. The only issue we had in the first year was the fact that she was never home and every time we made plans together, she was four to six hours late, or didn't show up at all. She was also at D and T's more then she was home, but when we were together, it was amazing. She would call me all the time; I loved to hear her voice. Funny, in the last two years we were together I had to beg her to call me, just to hear her voice.

At this time, she had built a small computer room off the front porch. I sat her down, looked into her eye's and told her that I was getting frustrated with never being able to spend time with her, always being cancelled on, always choosing to spend time with her friends and not me. I said that I have a tendency to just walk away when I am getting very frustrated and didn't want that to happen, I was very specific with her, I had to be in this relationship because I really liked her and didn't want it to end. I opened up to her and told her about how my mind works and how I react, she said she wanted someone who knew their mind and body and could communicate.

She said time meant nothing to her and she had no concept of it, if she felt like sitting at her friends and lost track of time, it wasn't on purpose it just happened. And nothing changed in the following weeks; she was still out at least five days a week, cancelling on me. I tried to talk to her a few more times over the next six to eight weeks but it never did any good. I was so infatuated with her that I couldn't bring myself to leave her.

One day she promised to be home early and it really looked like she meant it, she said she would be home by like nine that evening for us but she wasn't, I sat there until about three in the morning, waiting, again, and no show. I felt like a worthless piece of garbage. I left and went home to the motor home, I was so angry. That night I had enough and needed to end it. The next morning she was in the computer room visiting with some friends, I stormed in and started grabbing my stuff. Once I had it, I walked out. I think I said good-bye but was so steamed that she couldn't even get out of the room to come see what was wrong. She told me later that she and her friends could see I was angry before I entered the house but she sat there and visited instead, her friends were always more important than spending time with me and their opinions always carried more weight than mine, from day one.

It turns out it was her birthday the day I walked out. That bothered me when I realized it because I was looking forward to her birthday, how angry must I have been to completely forget her big day and focus her standing me up again. It was exactly one year to the day, the longest either of us had been in a relationship before the first fight. I went back the next morning to wait for a tow truck to tow my car out of her yard. She came out to see me; she was wearing the same PJ shirt, the pink one with black trim, which she wore the day we met. The sun was shining, she came up and we started talking.

In the middle of our talk, this guy, we will call him Lincoln. He was about five feet nine inches tall, medium length blond hair and was about one hundred and sixty pounds. He walked up behind her said hi and said she looked like she needed a hug. He did it with a kind of droopy face, immediately her arms went around him and they hugged, right in front of me while we were trying to work out our issues. After that he asked if she could help him out, she sold a little pot once in a while, she said yes to him and told me she would be right back. I was angry, frustrated, just downright pissed off but I did not let it show or control my thoughts. I wanted to be with her and it was the first real problem in a year, so I controlled it. She said she would make more time for us but she wanted to make us public, I said I wanted more time for just us. I said I didn't want a relationship where the parents were always yelling and arguing with the kids or in front of the kids, that is how I was raised and didn't like it. I didn't want a relationship like my brother's, always breaking up and getting back together for the same reasons, we needed to talk and take the each other seriously. She agreed and we got back together.

Everyone already knew about us anyways, they could see it when we were around each other, it was awesome. So we made it public. Later that day we started to talk about the future. I told her that I wanted us to have better life style, to quit smoking both cigarettes and marijuana. It would be much healthier for us. It was the same talk; we had several times in the previous year we were together and the ten months during the friendship. It is hard on my liver and it would give us a longer life together. The money we would save could do so much. We talked about trying to keep her power bills down by turning things off when they were not being used, living room TV, TV in Spunky's room, lights when not needed anything to bring down the bills a little. It never happened, lights and TV's were left on right until the day she dumped me.

We had this exact conversation so many times over the next few years also. The first time we talked about it was a major step toward falling in love with her, she said she wanted all those things for us, herself, her children and our future. From the day I met her, she said the smoking was going to be moved into the garage in the back once it got cleared out, after five years it was still packed solid. I mentioned several times over next four years to start by just moving the smoking outside. A smokeless house is better for everyone's health and it saves money because you will smoke less if you have to actually make more of an effort just to have one. Never once was it even tried, except when we broke up she tried and failed.

She said she wanted to have a long life with me and these were minor things to give up, or change. She was into body balancing, a type of massage/relaxation and was also into nutrition. We agreed to cut back on smoking and toking. I would buy the water and she was going to drink more of it to flush her system for the balancing. She said she needed to be in better health for it. She said she had to quit smoking pot during the day to stay clear headed, to focus. She said the balance wouldn't do any good if she wasn't looking after herself. We had planned a liver cleanse for over six months, through a break up even. Spunky was supposed to go to grandma's house for a weekend so we could do it but not even a week later, she was back to ditching me. It was even planned as far as knowing we had to give one or the other about one hour head start for the liver cleanse, so we weren't fighting over the bathroom. She kept cancelling until finally it became a figment of her imagination.

She went north for a weekend to take a course in her body balancing just after her birthday. A couple nights after she got back, we were laying in bed and I told her that I had fallen for her and wanted to look at spending the future together. She said she wasn't ready for a serious relationship and just wanted to have fun. I remember it vividly because I was laying on her looking down into her eye's. I was so hurt, after the talk we had just had a couple weeks earlier, the day after her birthday, I thought we were starting to get serious. I was wrong.

From the beginning she told everyone that I was making her quit smoking and toking, she used this against me so often. She told everyone that I was trying to change her, force her to change, force her to quit smoking and toking but it was our plan, for our future, as a family. She said she wanted to start her business. Never once did she really put in the effort to get it going. I had owned three businesses by that time but she never asked for help. She really seemed to want to get into it; she did all that studying, paid for those weekend courses, lined up a dozen clients, even more. She has the knowledge, and the forethought and the love for her studies to go far, especially with horses. Her studies allow her to be around horses and she said she loves that. A parent is supposed to make the changes that are needed, that they wouldn't normally do, for their children's well being. What makes a parent do what they want instead of what is best for the children? What stops a person from going after their dreams? Why do people give up on their dreams without really trying?

From the beginning, the kids were allowed in the smoke room and the door was always open. It was a major issue right from the start with us and was the cause of many arguments. When we met it was the spare bed room off the kitchen, then the computer room got built out of half of the front porch. The front porch ran the whole width of the house and was about five feet wide. When the computer room was built it was about five feet by up to twelve feet. There was a computer desk, a desk chair and three or four kitchen chairs stuffed into the room. Plus there was a large book shelve behind the door which opened inwards, it was a little cramped. There was even another chair available if needed outside the room. You get two or three people smoking in that room and it is terrible but when the door opens it all pours into the house. I have asthma; I always insisted that the window be open and the fan on, even during the winter. I was just as cold as everyone else and it was for every one's benefit but I took a lot of crap, a lot of times for opening that window.

The door was not solid to the computer room, it actually had a window that went about one foot from the edge of the door all the way around, so you could see in or out at any height. It had slightly tinted glass to look in the room but with a light or computer on, you can see clearly. Spunky used to stand there and watch us roll and smoke joints all the time, she and Kiddo would walk in at will, stand there with the door open while we were smoking or toking. Kiddo was her thirteen year old daughter. I tried like hell for six months to get something put on the window to block at least five feet and lower so Spunky couldn't see us, no way. Some cardboard got put up for a little bit but it was put on the outside of the door and Spunky had it down in no time. My opinions and concern's never meant anything, it was her house and her family, she said that numerous times. All I wanted was what was best for a family that wasn't mine.

I bought a canoe off of her that was sitting in her yard; she needed the money and said she loved the outdoors. I tried several times that second summer to get her out in the canoe with my brother and his kids, or just us. I said Spunky would have had a great time but she never wanted to go. She has this huge fire pit in the back yard, I tried to start holding BBQ and weenie roasts but she was never interested. All she did was go over to D and T's, when that fell apart she sat at home on the computer until the wee hours of the night.

I used to work on my cars in the back yard at Subject X's, I would bring Spunky to play outside and get some fresh air. I had to almost fight with Subject X to let me take her outside. The only time I had ever seen Subject X take Spunky outside was when she had something to do, not just to let Spunky play. She never came to the park the times Spunky and I went, she even dropped us off at a park once for an hour and went and sat at D and T's. The one time she came it was because she had gotten roped into it.

My brother's family, Spunky and I were planning on going to the park; Subject X had decided not to go. She had her friend from Saskatchewan come into town and when she found out we were taking the kids to the park, suddenly Subject X wanted to go, that really bugged me. It turned into one of those on again off again things for the next few years. When we were apart it was so brutal on me, almost every time we broke up it was for the exact same reason, she wouldn't make time for us. Over the four years we broke up at least six or seven times, only two of those were for different reasons. After we had broken up in the second year and were apart for about five months, Spunky, Subject X and her friend, we will call her Crosser, were on their way to the coffee shop. Crosser was an older lady about five feet two inches tall with blond hair and glasses. On their way to the coffee shop, Spunky asked if she started swearing again would I come by and wash her mouth out with soap. Subject X said she was amazed by her daughter and knew I was a good person to have in their lives, we should be together. We started talking again shortly after and got back together about two months later, which had been our longest break up.

About two months before we broke up Spunky started swearing. I gave her a warning and if she didn't stop she would get soap in her mouth. I wasn't rough and it was usually just a quick wipe, I only used the smallest amount for taste. Subject X only did it maybe two times in the three weeks it took to break that habit. I did it at least once a day, Subject X actually fought it at first but it had immediate results. And in less than three weeks she stopped swearing once and for all. Around this time she started saying she didn't want to be with someone who didn't want to get married, she always said it in front of her friends and she was not overly nice about it. So finally she was talking about an actual future. After some thinking on my part, I thought we could overcome our issues and opened my heart to her and her family and started to put future plans into action.

She was having a scare with cancer cells around this time, she had an operation set up for a couple weeks away, and we had just gotten back together. We couldn't have sex because of the operation before or after of course. At this time I started to tell her it wasn't about the sex, it was about just being alone with each other and spending one on one time. I mentioned this many times over the next year or so, I figured her experience with health issues and the thought that this could go bad, would change her attitude towards life, that she would want to do more, see that life is short, understand why I needed to quit my bad habits, a longer life with her, I was hoping she would see her own mortality in a better light.

Her mom had stayed for a few days before and after she went to the hospital, one of those days they had gone to a large grocery retailer in town to do some shopping. When they got back they were talking about how Subject X had made a comment about an attractive guy walking through the parking lot, loud enough for him to hear her. Then they realized his wife was sitting right there and they were embarrassed. We were just getting back together at the time and she is commenting on how hot another man is. I was hurt that it was just a big joke to her. I never once made any comment in front of her about any other woman, or mentioned how attractive another woman looked. If I saw an attractive woman I would look away, out of respect for the relationship I was in, I guess I have higher standards than most people.

In the spring of 2008, I started working with my brother; he was in construction so his body is more defined then mine. Subject X and B.M. used to ask him to take his shirt off. B.M. was about four feet ten inches tall, long blond hair, and very thin, rather petite with a very opinionated mouth. When my brother would leave the computer room they talked about who would ask him to take off his shirt. After a bit my brother said he felt uncomfortable about it and the sexual comments, she was my girlfriend. I mentioned it to her and she said too bad, if it was making him or me uncomfortable that was our problem. I asked her how does she think it makes me feel, she said she was just doing it to put my brother on the spot. Again, I let it go but it kept happening. My brother's visits became much less frequent.

When we got back together the last time, again we agreed there needed to be some changes, she wanted to start going out, socializing, dinners and movies. Ok, no problem, so did I. We tried to go for dinner; we got so close to the door. I brought in her mother to baby sit, gave her money for gas since she lived out of town. As we were about to leave Spunky got sick and we ended up going to the hospital until like three in the morning. We sat there for hours. She said thank you but that I didn't have to stay with them. I said of course I am staying, this is my responsibility also. I was showing her I would be there when she needed me, this was parenthood and I had no problem doing what was needed to be done. She said she really appreciated that. There is a difference sitting in a hospital all night then in front of the computer.

We went to her boss's wedding dinner, we got dressed up and went to her boss's Halloween party, I took her out of town for a couple days to the company yearly camping trip, and we did a lot of fishing. Even ran into Spunky's father out there on the first day. Fun. We did do more, I did more. I bought her flowers at least once a week, just a single red rose, once in a while a boutique. She still never made time for us alone as adults.

Her mother had a heart attack while we were broke up; she knows her parents are running out of time, her father can hardly walk. She wanted to be closer to them to help them in their last years. We talked and thought it was best to move to her parents, they live about an hour and a half west of here. We talked about options, she could sell her house or the smarter thing would be to tear it down and build a four plex. Sell three of them and keep one. Then buy a house were her parents live. A house that was smaller and only a ground floor, this was so we could just let them move in and we could move into their house. We would still each own our own houses but this way they wouldn't have to climb all those stairs, wouldn't have to move anything they didn't need. It was supposed to make life easier for her parents. I had no problem with moving closer to her folks to help them out. Subject X said her dad could get me a job at the mine driving truck, paid very well and regular hours. That was a good plan but nothing happened to head in that direction, again she withdrew from me.

Around this time in the relationship, I had just met a young kid, we will call him Partner. He was about twenty years old, six feet tall with dark short hair. He was half Dutch, very opinionated and liked to argue even if he was wrong, which was often. I gathered him and some other friends and we planned a day at the lake about two weeks ahead of time. Subject X said she was going to go, at the last minute she cancelled and stayed home, in front of the computer with her friends, that's where she was when I left and when I returned. We were gone all day and had a great time. Well not even three weeks later, her friend Lincoln asked her to go to the beach and she went with him, spur of the moment. When I found out I was pissed! Lincoln didn't understand why. When I explained that I tried to get her to come with a whole group of us and she cancelled at the last minute, but then he asked and ya sure, no problem. Then you could see he understood but she just blew it off like it meant nothing and went back to the computer.

We ended up moving in together. Things were supposed to change, again. We decided marriage was what we both wanted; it was time to settle down and work at becoming a family. I was working for a pizza place doing deliveries, the pay was good but I had to give a months' notice where I was living and needed to get caught up on some bills I had. She had a little money left over from a previous settlement. She had gotten one for around thirty thousand dollars a few months earlier from a car accident she was in a few years before we met. We were broken up at the time and by the time we got back together she went through most of it. She had enough marked off to do the renovations in the bathroom and a little left over.

I tried to get the computer moved into the living room, keep the smoking in the computer room. Connect the computer to the TV so we could watch movies from the net in the living room. It would cut down on the smoking and give us a place to sit as a family to hangout. She never even considered it.

I had developed an idea for an online company that offered a service, I had already invested five hundred dollars before we got back together and moved in together and she agreed to lend me the remaining five hundred the week I moved in. I needed on office space to get set up and work and do things. She had a spare room with nothing going on in it. It had a spare bed that Kiddo slept in when she was down visiting. I asked to use it as an office, she could set up her table in there also and we could work at different times, she said no way. I got stuck in the back side of our bedroom wedged between three dressers and a closet, not a lot of room. I had the printer in there; it was hard to organize anything. The idea was a good one but I could only invest the smallest amount into advertising one time and it got frustrating sitting in the bedroom closet area. All of my money went to pay house hold bills. The business failed. It should not have.

Around this time she said she was worried about my past financial situation, I had been sued a few times, had old bills across western Canada and numerous other transactions. She said she was worried that when we got married, her house would end up with leans on it from creditors; I needed to look at clearing up my past. I checked into it and filed for bankruptcy within a month so we could start over fresh together. I filed for bankruptcy because of her concerns, over the next year and a half she said numerous times that I only filed for bankruptcy for myself, so I could have a better future. That it had nothing to do with her, not for us. I am sure I would have filed sometime in the next few years but I did it at that time to ease her mind and it was the right thing to do for our future together. Of course it was always the same; she never made time for us except when I got off work late at night and after her friends left, never on my days off. We were living together and we still had no time alone. If anyone called in the morning she invited them over, even if we were curling up.

I was driving a car that had very limited brakes, the master cylinder had a valve on the back with a leak, brakes worked but you had to put over twenty times the pressure on the pedal and it couldn't lock up on asphalt. It needed to be boosted every time it started so I bought a power pack to boost it myself, I did replace the battery, put in a used alternator and a rebuilt starter, nothing fixed the problems starting the car and I couldn't afford to buy another one. It also had no heat because the heater motor didn't work, the outside drivers side handle broke so I had to leave the window down when I was out of the car. There was a fan that plugged into the lighter mounted to the dash so I could keep the windows defogged; it was a very cold winter. I also had no license at the time. When we moved in together I couldn't afford to fix it, bills first after all. I drove it for about eight months like that. We only lived together for about four months.

We came up with a monthly bill payment arrangement and wrote it all down on a calendar. Each week had one bill that got paid, three bills a month means we should have been caught up within three months, including paying off the electrician that wired her bathroom. I was smoking one pack of cigarettes a day, she was smoking a pack and a half a day, we were drinking two bottles of pop a day and we spent at least ten dollars a day on marijuana, that's over twelve hundred dollars a month. I talked to her several times and she would not cut back, if she and I cut back to three quarters of a pack each, bought a jug of water and 1 bottle of pepsi it would save so much.

Why should she, she says, she doesn't like being told what to do. She said she will spend her own money on smokes then. Things got even rougher after that.

Partner just started a new job and was trying to sell vacuums; he was in training for the job and wanted to give me a presentation. I said sure and he brought it over. At the beginning Subject X said she had seen it before, liked it, wanted one but she couldn't afford it. She went and sat in the computer room with Crosser. I went through it and was impressed by the unit, so impressed that I wanted one for the house, it was a four year deal at eighty dollars a month and since I wanted to show her that I will make commitments with her for our future, I signed up. It was the best; I wanted her to have the best. Also it was something she said she wanted and it came with twenty five years of access to a carpet shampooer. I got it and promised never to miss a payment, I have been late once but every time we broke up, even since we broke up this last time, I have sent her the money to put in her account for it, every time. I hate that vacuum. I sure wouldn't have spent four thousand dollars on it for myself.

I had done lots of sales in the past; I knew I could sell this unit. The company wasn't exactly on the level with clients when it came to setting up appointments. I went to work for the company, keeping my night job doing deliveries. I had to spend one hundred dollars on dress clothes for the job, which she threw in my face many times. Wasting one hundred dollars on a job I kept for three weeks but we were spending over twelve hundred dollars a month on garbage. That was almost half of what I was making driving around in the cold but I did it to provide for the household, like a man is supposed to, at any cost. I still couldn't get any alone time with her and we were living together.

Chapter 10

'Subject X Part 2'

It was Christmas time. For the whole year before, she had been complaining about how I never bought her any jewellery, she made it very public in front of her friends, to the point of belittling me. So that Christmas I bought her a ring, she gave me a stack of homemade adult coupons. I loved it! I didn't spend a lot on the ring but it was the first ring I bought anyone. I got it with life time sizing, once I knew her ring size I could surprise her in the future with one I could actually put on her finger. It took her eleven months to get it sized; it took her almost two weeks just to find it in her house to get it sized. I was exceptionally patient; I don't think another man would have been.

We started to talk about having a child. She said she would love to carry mine. I was amazed and flattered and looking forward to it. It was supposed to be a new beginning, new possibilities and tons of potential. Again she had that spark but it didn't last long and it was back to the usual. At Christmas time, Subject X got some board games; she said she wanted to start a game night. It was tried once, twice maximum and the rules in the games she chose were complicated. There were kids, the first game should have been simpler but the whole thing faded out very fast. And game night disappeared within two weeks.

I actually had developed two ideas for online businesses but the first one was so big and expensive to build, it was put on the shelf. I learned of a community contest that offered two thirds of the money I needed. The problem was the business plan had to be submitted within one month. I tried to work in the closet but it was so cold and cramped, that it didn't last more than a couple of days. So I sat in the living room on a nice comfortable chair in the corner. It took the whole month, it was a massive under taking and I got it handed in on time, just by a day or two.

When Subject X and I talked about her time on her computer, she always compared that to the time I spent working on my computer. I wasn't playing games or watching movies, I was racking my brain in numbers. A couple nights I needed to finish a thought or something in the paper work and got to bed half an hour or so later then her, she got right mad and said I was the one who would rather be one the computer and threw it in my face numerous times. I was working, trying to build something for the future. Just because I didn't win the contest does that mean it was a waste of time? Should I only try things I know will be a success? I would never try anything then, this is reality, not mine, it's just the way the world works.

One night after working doing deliveries, it was slow as hell, I got home and they were all in the living room watching a movie on Partner' laptop. I sat down and noticed she was low on smokes again, I only had a few. In the past two weeks it had become a major issue between us, if she would just cut back a little. So I didn't want to say anything in front of anyone, or maybe she was right and I did it to teach her a lesson but I had no money for smokes and she said she just borrowed ten dollars from B.M. for gas. She never asked me to put it in her car; I knew it wasn't for gas. She complains how I eat takeout while I'm working but not only is supper always around seven in the evening, I am at work by five, but she borrows money on our budget, so she can smoke.

She always cooked food I didn't care for. Over half of the time she cooked this yorkshire pudding cake, the meat was sliced up and put inside of the dough. I told her many times that I liked my meat not to be cooked in a sauce or dough, just spiced and plain, maybe BBQ sauce. She never once cooked some meat off to the side for me. I used to cook the kids and I pancakes for breakfast, she didn't like pancakes, she liked eggs. I offered every time to cook her some eggs and did a few times but she never took that consideration when cooking for me.

In the morning we were both out of smokes and I would not give her ten dollars to go to the store to buy some, I had two days off and twenty dollars. She freaked out and went to the store with her ten dollars; she got back and was storming around. For a change I asked her for a smoke, she said NO! I said what, she repeated NO! I never once turned her down for anything if I had it on my person; I have gone to the store in the middle of the night many times for her. I was pissed off, I packed my stuff and left. I have to work in those conditions, in that car with no heat in the winter and she can spend, spend, spend or smoke, smoke, smoke. I wouldn't have been edgy all the time if we had some alone time but even living together, we were never alone. During the day when Spunky was in school, all we did was sit in the computer room and when we did go lay down it was for a nap and that was it. Never time for a little intimacy. From the moment I had gotten those adult cards for Christmas, I had tried to use them but after two months, I had only used maybe six of them, but tried over two dozen times.

It was heartbreaking leaving that day, Subject X and Spunky sat in the computer room crying. Spunky was asking why I was leaving, didn't I love them? Subject X said no, he is leaving, I was so torn up. Doesn't she want more out of life then smoking pot with her friends and playing on the computer? She said she did. I told her on my way out that I would start paying her back the money she lent me for my online business within a couple weeks and although most of her friends said I was a con man and would never pay, I paid back every cent, when I said I would.

She went on the social networking site and posted how after so many years she finally trusted someone and used her house as collateral on a vacuum. Then it said she got conned into keeping and paying for the vacuum and then she posted my name as the con man. That was the start of all my hatred for that vacuum that is what started me using the vacuum to piss her off. She never did see what it truly represented. When I moved out I didn't even take the vacuum with me, I left it behind for her house, and I never said I wouldn't make the payments. I would pay back the five hundred dollars but not pay the eighty dollars a month for the vacuum? I gave my word and even though we were not together I had every intention of making the payments but again she never even gave it a chance to fail, she just jumped to her own conclusion but I have made every payment since.

At this time Partner was bringing his laptop over almost every night to stream movies. This happened for a couple months before we broke up. When he broke up, I had to ask Partner if he had slept with her, he said no. She was making more time to watch movies with him then time to spend with me, who wouldn't wonder? That couple months was the longest time we sat in the living room with people to watch movies or do anything in five years. Around this time, she stopped calling me all the time, lucky if she called three times a week; unless she needed a favour or I was late after work.

Again we ended up back together and again talked about change, not even a week and things went back to the same with her. I was really starting to get frustrated at this point. I wanted to quit smoking pot but how when the one you're with is smoking it all day sitting on the computer. I got a job hauling manure and quit smoking pot, I had to quit in case of a drug test. It was a decent paying job. With it, we talked again about future plans and stuff. We talked about how in three pay checks I could afford to pay for her divorce and we could look at getting married, she looked excited. She said she realized she was looking at life as a glass half empty sort of thing and she said she wanted to be a glass half full kind of person like me. She wanted to get into her balancing and nutrition. We talked about a healthier lifestyle, a more active and social life. We did go out a few times to events we were invited to, I bought her flowers again and tried to take her out. She came to family BBQ's and hung out a few times with everyone.

Again, not one balance, not one attempt at cutting back or quitting smoking or toking, no change in diet or eating and sleeping habits and of course still no time for us. I offered to pay for her quit smoking prescription she said she had for over six months, she said at eighty dollars it was too expensive. I said at twenty five dollars a day it is well worth it. She said it was easier to come up with that day then dish out eighty in one shot.

During the last couple weeks before we broke up yet again, the smoking and toking thing was a big problem. I was especially getting tired of Spunky seeing us do it. The reason we broke up this time was not for the normal reason, no adult time. This time it was for smoking pot in front of her daughter.

Subject X's friend B.M. would never keep her mouth shut. I could never have a conversation with Subject X without her sticking her two cents in. In the last six months of the relationship, she would show up around five in the evening and as soon as she walked in she would say she didn't have to pick up her daughter from work until ten that night, so she wasn't leaving until then. It happened at least three times a week, especially on my days off. Subject X never said anything, even when we had planned for a quiet night, her friend came first.

B.M.'s house had flooded from a massive amount of rain that fell. She said she had all these scale model cars, she said she would sell them to me for five dollars apiece if I could come help, of course I agreed. I liked those cars and although I didn't care for the lady, she was a good friend of Subject X's. I always wanted to start a collection, they were her ex-husbands and she wanted them out of the house anyways. The basement was packed full of boxes, there was a bedroom set up in the corner. Everything had to be moved so the carpet could be removed. The septic tank kept flooding into the downstairs shower.

Her ex-husband was in jail for domestic violence and doing ten years. He is supposed to be getting out in the next year or so. I have never met him, and that is all I will say about it. He had filled in all the ditches with dirt it flooded the ditches at every heavy down pour. And this was a very heavy down pour over a few days. It took about eight or nine hours and it was disgusting, the septic tank backed up into the house over and over again. When all was said and done, she changed it to thirty five dollars a car and I only picked seven cars, which in the end I gave back. Subject X heard her say the original deal the first time but kept her mouth shut when the deal changed.

B.M. had this huge property just outside the city and she was in trouble with the city a few months later. She had these brushes that were about six feet high and it was about half the size of a soccer field. Lots of work had to be done and it was put off until the last week. Subject X, Spunky and I went out there the first day. We were all in the living room; Spunky was two feet from the coffee table sitting on the floor playing with the kitten. B.M. was sitting on the couch across from Spunky, Subject X was to her right on the couch and I was in the chair to the right of her. B.M. started rolling a couple joints right in front of Spunky, she rolled two. Then she lit one and I was just pissed but I said nothing, I knew the responses I would get. Right in front of a five year old kid, who is starting school, who likes to talk a lot. Bad news. I believe we smoked the second one in the garage. Then we went to work. You are right, I could have taken Spunky and gone outside but what good would it have done? When I am not around they do it anyways.

I had brought two weed whackers with me that I had borrowed. I used one and Subject X used the other. After about a half hour, I could see this wasn't working. The brush was too much for these machines, I could not afford to repair them if they broke and one of them would have. I was pissed at the fact that B.M. could afford to buy marijuana but couldn't afford to get the right equipment for the job, a job she would have gotten nailed hard by the city if it wasn't done. I said I wasn't wrecking this equipment and we had to stop using it. I said I would run back into town and rent the machine because I wasn't repairing these ones. Subject X got real mad out at me because I said it was stupid that she could afford drugs but couldn't get the equipment. Finally I couldn't take the stupidity on her part defending her friend and got in the jeep and went and rented a commercial weed trimmer, plus bought a steal blade which made things so much easier. It cost about seventy dollars, I was only left with a little money but it had to be done.

I got back out to her place, it was about half past one in the afternoon or so and I had to work at five. I busted my hump getting as much done as possible but I had to leave by quarter to four. Subject X took over and I went to get ready for work. During the evening between deliveries, I had stopped at her house to talk to her. I was completely calm, sat down beside her in the computer room, we were alone, I made her get off the computer and look at me. I looked into her eye's and said that this rolling joints and smoking pot in front of Spunky must stop, she is starting school, she always has to be part of the conversation. What if they talk about drugs at school? She agreed on that point and said she would make sure it didn't happen again. We talked for a bit more about it, I wanted to make sure she understood how important this was. She said she agreed no more in front of Spunky.

Subject X, my mom, my step dad and I had all been baptized in the last month, or so, at a church we had joined. The next day we were going back out to B.M.'s to finish up. So my mom came with use to help out on the weeding part of it. We got there; we all went into the house and sat down. Again B.M. started to roll joints, in front of Spunky, sitting three feet away on the floor. Subject X just looked at me and shrugged her shoulders in the slightest of ways. I was so pissed; she couldn't do what was right, stand up to her friends to do what was right by her own daughter. My mom was shocked also, we had all just been baptized, all trying to cut back, mom had quit and didn't want to be around it. She was there to help B.M. and no respect was shown. I think we lit it outside by the front door, my mom and Spunky went off to dig. We got half way through it and B.M. put it out, thought that was odd. So I went and fixed the trimmer because right after I left the day before the blade shifted and Subject X couldn't fix it. I started working and was powering through it in record time. About forty five minutes later I looked up and there was Subject X and B.M. standing there smoking the other half of that joint.

Spunky was playing in front of them, about twenty feet away. It was hot, I am busting my hump, paid for the equipment to do the job on someone else's yard and not once has anyone offered water and they are standing there smoking a joint in front of Spunky. I was so angry! I just wanted the job done before I got stuck paying for another twenty four hours. I still can't believe the total disregard for everything and everyone, even her own daughter.

That night we broke up again, for the first time I told her "If you can't do right by your own daughter, how can I expect you to do right by us?" Those were my exact words; I made sure I stated it as simple and to the point as possible. She said I was forcing her to do something and I don't have the right, it's her life, her family, her house. All I wanted was what was best for her daughter. How can a boyfriend/ fiancé/husband want what's best for a child that is not his and the biological mother not care or see what is happening? How could I, someone who never wanted kids until meeting her, let someone suck me in and spit me out so many times and she thinks she is the victim.

I had started a new job hauling manure in a town close by. I quit smoking pot, in case of a drug test and I had just been baptized. We started talking again and after a couple weeks and got back together. She got baptized within a couple weeks. I was working six days a week, Monday to Friday twelve hour shifts and eight on Saturday. It was a one hour round trip to and from work, and then there was a ten to twenty minute wait until we got loaded into vans a headed to the job site, usually within a ten minute drive. Then letting the trucks warm up and clean the boxes of left over manure was about fifteen minutes with the daily check. I would get back to town about quarter to eight in the evening. One hour to eat and shower, it left me about one and a half hours until bed. I called her on my way back to town one night, it was a Thursday and said I was tired and just wanted my bed. She said that worked, B.M. and Lincoln were visiting because he was moving to Saskatchewan and they were saying good bye. Ok I thought and then I said I will talk to you tomorrow at the same time and we will get together and spend some time alone, she said yep and we hung up.

The next night at the same time as every night, I called her after work and let her know I was off work and headed into town, I was going home to eat and shower. I showered, ate and called her at about twenty to nine, I told her I would be by in about twenty five minutes. She said great see you then; she called back ten minutes later asking if I could pick her up a pack of smokes on my way. I said sure, no problem. As I was pulling up, I saw the grandmothers' car and Lincoln's car. Once I got in front of the house I could see her smoking a joint with him, the grandmother must be in the living room with Spunky.

Then as I am getting out of the jeep, I see her light incense and start waiving it around. I walked in and it reeked like pot. She was in the computer room with Lincoln and I couldn't go in there, it was hard enough to quit without being that close to it. The grandmother was in the living room with Spunky, like I thought, so there was no place for us to visit and hangout. Again I am pissed and give her the smokes and walked out. She knew the day before when exactly I was going to stop by and only had an hour and a half, there was a house full and Spunky was wide awake. Again no time for the adults.

I was up at half past five for work, it wasn't easy. I didn't sleep the night before, I was rather frustrated. The next three hours were just brutal, but at eight thirty I had to call her. I should have waited until I got off work but what can I say, I was exceptionally frustrated. She had just started working for a friend of hers; we had gone to his wedding dinner. It was the first and only job she had in the five years I knew her; the job was outdoors doing odd jobs. She hadn't been there long and it was Saturday morning when she answered the phone, I started right off with the reason why I was so pissed off, she said this is her day off and I call her like this, then she hung up. I believe there were calls or emails back and forth for a couple days but we broke up, again, for the exact same reason, no time for us.

For two weeks my mom tried to get a hold of Subject X to return a woman's bible that belonged to her. My mom got a hold of her twice and both times, a time and day was set to pick it up but she never showed. Then she stopped answering the phone calls, returning emails, she just played dead. Her boss is a Christian, owns his home and runs a handyman type of a business. He also smokes a little pot. When Subject X came home from work, she did tell me about her day but she always mentioned the joints they smoked, she didn't have to tell me they smoked one or two before, during and/or after work, why would I need that info? She also said they talked about religion, faith and the bible, he went to bible school.

She and I had been baptized about two months earlier, in a church I still feel is the closest thing to the right church. So she read the bible, in record time, I was impressed. She read two other books people gave her, to say she did. As soon as she was done, it was back to the computer. She started with this attitude all of a sudden about how anything in moderation is ok for you. I mentioned to her then a line of coke, or a hit of smack, or a hit of acid in moderation would be ok, she said yes! As long as you control it.

After a week or so, I had to get a hold of her boss/friend; he had said he was interested in checking out our church with his wife in the weeks before we broke up. I wanted to find out what he said to her to make such drastic changes in her belief that God would think it is ok to do any drugs in moderation. I ended up contacting him on his birthday through a social network, I asked him to call me. We talked on the phone and in the conversation it came up about how she was avoiding us and my mom was trying for over a week to return the woman's bible that she lent her.

Well he and his wife had given the bible to subject X. I mentioned that I had talked to my minister and he would like to sit down and discuss this point of view on whether it was ok to smoke pot in moderation as a Christian. Her boss went to bible school, I didn't, and I agreed with my minister, I wanted to fight knowledge with knowledge. If I tried to explain what I believe, who was I? I didn't go to bible school. He got angry, said what he said behind his closed doors, stays behind closed doors. Is that the way a true Christian behaves? Why would a true Christian need to talk behind closed doors? If he is talking about what he believes to someone, doesn't that person have the right to check it out? And if that someone changes the way they think, does the spouse not have the right to ask questions? Does the spouse not have the right to figure out where this all came from? Should he even have talked about religion with someone without including their spouse, or respect his side? Ya we were broke up, but I wanted answer's.

I wanted to have religious discussions with him, with our minister; fighting knowledge with knowledge was the best way to do it. The funny part, he said from his studies, he learnt back in Jesus' time that they smoked hashish while fasting to curb their appetite. Are you kidding me! THC of any kind makes you hungry, why would you use something that is going to make you hungrier if you are fasting? She told everyone that I was trying to force her to quit again, smoking and toking. Sorry for trying to be healthier, sorry for not wanting to smoke pot in front of her daughter. When I talked to her boss he asked me what gives me the right to use the law to force her to quit smoking anything. I was flabbergasted! Why? Listen to what happened to him a couple months earlier.

He was having the same issue with his wife. He was a non smoker and she was a smoker. After they were married, they talked and she agreed to stop smoking. One day he drove by her work for a surprise lunch, she was outside smoking, he was pissed off. He was angry and had a right to be. Why didn't I? Just because they didn't know about my health issue? What gave him the right to say anything after what he went through with his wife? Why did she say one thing to me but the opposite to her friends? It gets better.

The next day Subject X called and screamed and hollered at me because she said he got really mad at her for not caring enough about the gift, the woman's bible, to go see my mom and get it back. She said that he said, it was disrespectful and she should get it back, it was a gift from him and his wife. She said he was so mad at her over this book that she almost lost her job. It was ridiculous. Up until this point, four years, she never accused me of going through her friends to get her in trouble or created any problems for her in our many break ups, never once. Wouldn't a true Christian say something like, you must do what you think is best; here let me buy you another book. What is it five, ten, fifteen, twenty, or even forty dollars, what is money to a Christian? I wanted answers that time with her boss but she still thinks and always thought I did it to get to her.

She had sent me an email saying if I didn't stop causing problems with her boss/friend she would charge me with slander. I said then she would just be ratting herself out. I said if I had to go in front of a judge and make a statement as to why I did what I did and I would have the right to defend myself in a court of law, it would be because of smoking pot and that would bring in child welfare. I wasn't going to lie under oath for her. She freaked again and said how dare I threaten her with child welfare but she would be doing it to herself. Yet again, she was the victim. I did it because I wanted and needed answers, just like now, I want and need answers but not only do I know this time that she will never tell me the truth, I know there was nothing more I could have done. And that hurts, all the effort I put in and I couldn't even get one day alone with her in a week, let alone two weeks. This was fall of last year.

Again we got back together, I was still working hauling manure but the season was coming to an end. I took Subject X and Spunky out for dinner and mini golf one Saturday night. The next Saturday, I took her to dinner and a movie. I was so happy to be out with her that a homeless lady came up and asked for change for soup, I gave her ten dollars in loonies and said something like have more than soup. Still she made no time for us during that month at night, no romantic evening, and no afternoon cuddling, absolutely nothing.

I tried again to get the pot smoking to be outside. I started to smoke again and when I went over to visit her I would go outside on the back patio to smoke it. She asked me if I was too good to smoke it with her in her house. I told her I was doing it to show her it would be better, she just got mad every time I did it and after a week I gave up.

I wasn't doing deliveries any more so I said that on the Saturdays that Spunky was with her father, we would go out to dinner and a movie, go out and enjoy ourselves. On the Saturdays she was home, we would make it a family day, go out just the three of us and do something to tire Spunky out so we could have a quite night at home. She said no, that was like keeping track of whose turn it was to do something. I tried to explain this is what a family does; they work around the life they got. Saturday nights made sense, it didn't mean we couldn't do something else and be spontaneous any other day but at least Saturdays would be for the family or for us. It wasn't a good enough start for her, yet she had no suggestions or ideas. She said that it felt like it was keeping track of who's turn it was on Saturdays and she didn't want to do it.

This time she was finally ready to give counselling a try, I had been mentioning it for almost a year before. We started by seeing a counsellor and joined a program to help family's be closer. It was a good course but, again, it didn't change anything. About half way through the counselling, she started so say she didn't want any more kids, she would be too old to enjoy life by the time they were eighteen. She said that was final. Again she was pulling away but I followed.

Just before we joined the course I borrowed two thousand dollars from my boss. I was back doing deliveries, got laid off from hauling manure. Winter was just starting and I knew with my jeep I could make money by putting a snowplough on it. So I borrowed the money went to the store and paid for it. They said it would be here in about two weeks. When the two weeks was up, they said at least two more weeks, demand was high out East. After that they said two more weeks, I returned the receipt and got my money back. I ended up with a flat deck trailer five feet wide and eleven feet long. I also bought a riding lawn tractor with a snowplough on the front.

I made some money with it but there wasn't a lot of snow fall at this time, so I tried to figure out a way to diversify the equipment I got, which was just the jeep and trailer. So I started a recycling company. I would pick up washers, dryers, stoves and dishwashers for free and any miscellaneous steel as long as the customer loads it. I landed contracts with a few appliance stores, placed some ads. It had great potential and is still running.

I talked to Subject X and asked her if she would like to be a partner. I had, or could get, the equipment and she had the room. I said I would redo the back gate so it was chain link and electric so a car door opener would open it and she could park in the back to avoid damage and break-ins to her car. I also said I would build another fence to separate the yard from the parking area. I'd make the parking lot in the back gravel; I would buy a couple more trailers so excess steel could be stored without being on the ground in the yard. It would increase the value of property, bring in an income, give us a job we can both do and could take Spunky so we didn't need to pay a babysitter. I asked her to think about it for two or three days and get back to me. I made sure I was specific with her to think about it and get back to me within three days tops.

Four days later, I had to ask her. She was avoiding something as simple as a yes or no. She said she didn't want all the mess of loose steel in her yard. I said there would be two or three smaller trailers to sort it in and nothing will be on the ground. And then she said how would we divide it if we split up. That thought never even crossed my mind, we were planning to get married, if she was thinking like that, then she knew she didn't want to be with me, why did she bother to agree to get back together? Or go to counselling?

This year I started an Electric Lawn Company with Partner. We were in a tool store looking at machines and we ran into her boss and an employee. He started a conversation, Partner did most of the talking, I wasn't overly friendly but not rude. They did their thing, we did ours. After we paid I was hungry and we walked to a fast food place across the parking lot. And there they were again, ordering lunch. I was thinking I could have been nicer, he doesn't know the truth. So I started a conversation, we talked about promoting each other with flyers, I told him he should stop by and see our tractor, he said one day. We exchanged flyers and everything seemed fine and friendly. I have given his number out and will continue to do so.

I did a TV news interview to promote the business; I posted a link to it on the social network. Her boss clicked the like button. A week later or so, I found out about this group of business owners that meet once a week for breakfast and discuss their businesses, exchange business cards and promote each other. It looked like something he would be interested in. I sent him a message through the social site letting him know about it. He never did reply.

She said she was ready but she is still holding her marriage as a blue print, as an excuse to do what she wants, when she wants and no man will tell her what to do. Even if it is a mutual agreement, she feels like she is forced into changing but isn't the other person changing also? Aren't you both making sacrifices?

She got pregnant at an early age, she was so worried about what her family would say, and she asked her friends to find her someone to marry. They did and she got married to someone she didn't know just to keep her family off her back. In no time he moved them out of town and started beating her. He was quitting his jobs and they were moving all the time, they lived in disgusting places. One place didn't even have a washroom, it just had an outhouse. She had no friends, wasn't allowed to go out, and was barely allowed to breath. I have confirmed all this, so I know it's true. They still communicate on subjects when it comes to Kiddo, as they should.

With this experience she surrounds herself with anyone who will visit her at any time. It is the reason she says whatever to end a serious conversation, it is why she does what she wants when she wants, she has the freedom and she doesn't want to give it up, even if it is the right thing to do for her family, it must be her idea otherwise it is no good.

Her husband did a real number on her. That is why after over twelve years of separation, she is still married to him, and it is an excuse not to have to get serious in a relationship. She can't get remarried and has done nothing to work on her divorce. She has gotten two settlements over the last ten years worth over forty thousand dollars and still couldn't pay the five hundred to complete the divorce.

In the end, all the rules she said I tried to enforce or change were things we had discussed at great length and came to an agreement on. Isn't that a partnership? For one of these reasons, financial, health, emotional and/or physical improvement for our family. On her end nothing ever changed, when I was working at any job she never set an evening aside for us, even on my days off. However, when she started work her hours changed and suddenly she was complaining about me not making time, I was working sixty hours a week and when I did stop by she was getting high and had people over.

Out of four years in that relationship, she only spent two nights at my place and that was only because we were renovating her bathroom. She demanded that I spend the nights with her at her place but again she didn't have to put in the effort. We never had a quite night when Spunky was gone for the weekend, or even the day. It is amazing what you don't see in a relationship just to make it through to the next day, week, month, and year. That is no way to live.

CHAPTER 11

CHAPTER 11

KIDS AND IN-LAWS

This chapter is about Subject X's kids and the in-laws. I care for both of the kids a great deal. When I met them, Spunky was still in diapers, about two years old, Kiddo was about thirteen. They all lived in a three bedroom, one bath house, no upstairs and an open dirt basement. Subject X bought it about six years earlier with a settlement from her first big car accident. Each child had their own room but for some reason Subject X slept on a double mattress, box spring and wooden bed frame with drawers in the dining room for around three years while I knew her and for at least two years earlier.

The kids had their own room but the third room was stuffed full and there was a TV and a couch to sit on. If that wasn't enough, there were kitchen chairs that could be used. This was the only room that we sat in, or watched TV in, until the computer room was built in the first eight months of us seeing each other, before the blow out on her birthday. The computer was bought around the fifth month of seeing each other; once it was in the house the computer room was built. She stayed sleeping in the living room for at least another year and a half.

When she and Spunky's dad, we will call him Relaed, hooked up she already had bought her house. He was into selling narcotics, more and different stuff then I did. I heard stories of piles, bags and stacks, sounded crazy. I got all this information over the years from different people. This was all in her house with children and it was all the time.

After awhile, they planned to have a child together. According to her it was all planned out and they were going to make a family together.

100

She said they had talked about it but she wasn't able to get pregnant for the last ten years, so the odds weren't good. And then came Spunky. From my understanding he was cheating on her before she got pregnant and she knew it, she just didn't want to admit it. So they had a child together. The lifestyle and income stayed the same. Fancy meals, camping and fishing with the best equipment, the typical stuff when living that way.

Things went downhill from there, more parties in the back garage, more narcotics everywhere; the garage had been broken into a couple of times, just the normal spiral that follows that lifestyle. At this point I believe she had something like four other people living in her house plus her and the two kids. There were also at least two big dogs. He would take off and go get drunk with his friends, go camping all the time with or without her and would just disappear on her for hours or days. And there were always girls around him. He did what he wanted when he wanted and rarely asked if she wanted to join him. She stayed at home with the kids and he went out.

One week during the summer, she and the kids went to her folks, leaving everyone else at her house. They had a pig roast and left the leftovers there until she got back. It was stunk fiercely and was full of maggots. They had to light a massive fire for hours to burn the ground because all the grease and fats of a decomposing pig.

Relaed was always in the back garage getting drunk and high and making oil from the shake. Believe this, four years after I met Subject X she was still finding garbage bags of old marijuana and viles of oil, from inside the garage, to the basement of her house. The last time was last year when renovating the bathroom. If she would have got busted any time in that four years she would have lost her house for sure.

Relaed was in jail when I met Subject X, he had been there for at least a year and a half. He got out about two years ago. He was arrested for something along the lines of possession with intent, proceeds from crime and possession of stolen property. He did about four years. He got out and moved to a small town just outside the city. After a couple of months Kiddo went to live with him, she moved from the ex-husband's place. Spunky visited him every second Saturday from about ten in the morning till eight at night. He had to pick her up and drop her off. Sometimes she would come back early if she was sick or even a couple times her behaviour was more than they could deal with.

Since he got out, he wasn't working and when he paid his child support he had a stack of cash. We all knew he was back in the game, it was a discussion Subject X and I had when Kiddo went to move in there but what could we do, she was almost seventeen and legally she had the right to choose. From our understanding there was alcohol and drugs in the house, parties, sex where ever and Kiddo walked in on one or two of them. In the end, he ended up back in jail and got a couple more years. He will bounce in and out for the rest of his life I am sure. He enjoys the lifestyle too much. What a way to watch your daughter grow up. What a way for a daughter to see her father, visiting him behind bars because that lifestyle is more important to him.

His mother, the Grandmother, had white hair about a foot past the shoulders, wore glasses and was about five feet four inches tall. S he was a little heavy set, but just a little. She was no different, she has been arrested more than her son and once it was a hair away from Spunky going to child welfare. Subject X had allowed Grandma to take her out for dinner. On the way back she had cut off a pedestrian and a cop saw it. As she was pulling up out front, the cops turned on his lights, Subject X went out and Spunky came running from the car crying. When Grandma went into her purse, a bunch of pills from a baggy fell out and that gave the cops probable cause to search her car. They found pills, marijuana, cash and more on her and in the car. This was just before Spunky's father got out of jail.

After this, child welfare got involved and said the Grandma was no longer allowed to be alone with Spunky. Subject X knew about the drugs in the car, it was always there and she knew it. I warned her a long time before it was going to happen, she just got lucky and it happened out front of her house instead of a street were child services would have shown up. Spunky is talkative and open, it could have been bad but Subject X doesn't recognize the potential for disaster. And it is so close.

The first two or three years we were together, Grandma would come over almost every evening between eight and ten and would stay until at least three hours. Subject X and I talked about it; she knew Grandma was just doing it so we wouldn't be alone. Subject X said she was doing it so that when Relaed got out they, might get back together. Subject X said that would never happen but because Grandma does and buys so much she should be able to visit whenever she wanted. It cut back a little in the last year but only the number of visits, not the hours, even with school. Subject X uses her like a bank, when ever Spunky wanted something; she dialled the phone for her.

The grandmother is a pack rat. Grandma's house was completely cleaned out about seven years ago and is just packed full again, so the story goes. She would buy cases of stuff that was about to expire, mayo, frozen squash, cereals, countless food items, other things, toys, clothes and anything you can think of. Subject X had two boxes of chocolate honey combs in her cupboards for the last three years at least, they were expired when I first saw them, they were there the day we broke up and I will bet they are still there. Grandma pay's for the satellite TV that is wired into the living room. Subject X said the satellite is for Spunky so she can watch the TV whenever and watch whatever she wants. In the five years I knew Subject X, the only time I was allowed to watch TV was when Spunky was gone or in bed. The living room belonged to Spunky, she did all her crafts, beading, TV watching and movie watching in there and still does, I am sure. I said let's just put the satellite in her room and I would pay for cable, no way the living room is the play room, period. There was nothing in the house that she wasn't allowed to play with. Subject X had figurines, glass, porcelain, silverware and lots of wolf stuff, if Spunky got mad enough, she got it or went and took it.

After I gave up the delivery business, Kiddo stayed home a lot by herself playing on the computer and I sat in the living room watching TV, waiting but Subject X and Spunky were always out at D and

T's until the late hours of the night, five to seven days a week. She got home so late and I was done work around three in the morning, I spent a lot of nights over there visiting with kiddo, or just sitting watching TV, waiting for their arrival. It wasn't very busy at night so I sat at her place while Kiddo was in the computer room.

At this time, we had discussed, again, living better. Supper as a family, healthier lifestyle, earlier nights, all the usual stuff in that conversation. She rarely cooked meals, was usually quick throw together meals. Spunky ate more chicken noodle soup, white rice and McDonald's then any kid I that have ever met. In our second year together, she said the second worse thing I have ever heard a mother say and she said it in front of her kids. We had gone shopping a couple days earlier and of course she didn't freeze the meat like she was supposed to. Just put it in the fridge and left it, well there were two roasts, they had to be cooked. We agreed she would cook one that day and I would cook the other the next day.

I pitched in on the grocery bill all the time when I was included in meals, her friends think I was just eating her food and called me a mooch a few times. I didn't tell them when I helped out on the food bill, it's not their business, and I didn't need their gratification. Little did I know, Subject X just agreed with her friends instead of telling the truth, why else would she call me a mooch unless she agreed.

She cooked a nice meal, no complaints that night, it was a great roast. However, I have professional experience and tons of advice when it comes to cooking and I started cooking at a young age. So the next day when I cooked, while we were dishing out our plates, Kiddo had tasted the roast, I don't think she thought about what she was saying but she said this roast was so much better than her mom's the night before. Subject X immediately said that's why I don't cook for my kids, never good enough! Those were her exact words; I couldn't believe what I just heard!

Spunky woke up almost every night, her room was so packed full of toys over the first few years it was just easier on Subject X to let her have the living room. She slept on the couch four to six nights out of a week, with the TV on all night. When she did sleep in her room, the TV was also on all night and loud. She was put to bed in her mom's bed four to six nights a week and always had to be moved for us to go to bed. And all the other nights she woke up and crawled in. The child did this from the time I met them right until the end. A six year old in school, a six year old needs proper sleep, a six year old needs good nutrition and so much more. All I ever tried to do was what we agreed on, what was best for the family, for the child.

The relationship between Kiddo and her mom was not a healthy one. They always screamed and yelled back and forth. After about two and a half years Kiddo moved in with Subject X's ex-husband . . . oops they are still married, I guess he isn't an EX yet. Before that, it was bad and Spunky saw it all and behaved in the same manner. Once Kiddo moved Spunky's attitude got a little better, she wasn't yelling as much.

Kiddo spent a lot of nights sitting at home by herself in the first two and a half years I was around. Subject X and Spunky were out all night, every night at D and T's sitting around visiting. Kiddo stayed at home on the computer every night, and then in the second year she had serious problems with people on the internet. Gee, no computer, no problems, one year with a computer and she was in all kinds of crap. Talking to people she shouldn't have been and just pissing off who ever she wanted. The social network isn't as safe as some may think it is.

When Kiddo came to visit you, I could see a major change in her attitude toward the house, her sister and her mother. It was nice to see. She spent time with her sister; she talked to her mom, not yelled. She still thought she could do whatever she wanted, she was sixteen, what do you do at that point. She was actually getting into more trouble with people over the social network and it caused problems with Kiddo and the ex-husband. Kiddo moved back to Southern Alberta and moved in with Spunky's father.

I regretfully did get a little rough with Spunky once and felt bad for letting myself get that mad. It was about a year and a half after we started seeing each other. I was watching her for a couple hours. She was throwing this massive tantrum, I gave her two or three warnings that if she didn't calm down, and I was going to put her in her room. That didn't work, I gave her the warnings then went over and picked her up, I was gentle but as I was just standing up, she started to kick and throw her fists and she kicked me in the privates.

I have learnt from past experience when this happens, if possible finish what you are doing before the pain kicks in and you can't walk. So I held her tight so she couldn't move, took her to her room and dropped her on her bed and waited for it. It was a little painful but she didn't get a direct shot, I was lucky. I wasn't overly rough with her but I learnt not to pick her up that way and to operate more calmly with her, or any child.

Kiddo and I had one time when voices were raised. Subject X and Spunky were at D and T's and I was at her place, waiting for them as usual. I do not remember what was said but Kiddo said something rude and went into the computer room. I was steamed that a fifteen year old could talk to an adult that way. She came out about forty five minutes later and I think I asked her what that was all about. We talked for about five minutes and resolved it; she apologized and didn't realize that what she said had gotten to me. After that there was not another issue.

Those were the only two times I had serious issues with her kids, both times I learnt something and so did they, even if they didn't know it. Around this time I was getting very frustrated with all the yelling between her and the kids, especially Kiddo. And because of it, Spunky was yelling more. I had told her that was how I was raised and screaming at them doesn't solve the issue. If she spent less time in the computer room and more time out in the house with her children, attitudes and behaviours would change. I also said and my exact words were you're kids behave like monsters but they have the potential to be angels. I wasn't saying her kids were monsters but that's how she took it and threw it in my face until the very end. She always heard what she wanted. I said if the screaming, fighting, stomping and slamming doors were to stop, there wouldn't be so much stress around. It didn't change until Kiddo moved out. And even that was limited. How can you see a child's interaction and behaviour's when you are always in the other room, door opened or closed.

The children got whatever they wanted, all they had to do was call grandma and they got it. If Spunky said she wanted McDonald's all she had to do was ask mom to call grandma and in no time it was delivered, nine times out of ten. Spunky has more toys in her room than any other kid I have ever met. Maybe more than me and my brothers and sisters had combined. She has so much; it has made her materialistic and greedy. When people come over to the house, she was always asking what they brought her. She threw tantrums for a while when people came over without something for her. It took a while to break that attitude. She is such a sweet kid though, I've never met a child like her and I'm not likely to ever meet one like her again. Everyone who has met her says the same thing, she truly is one in a billion that one. I am going to miss her very much and her sister of course. I was looking so forward to teaching her things and watching her grow up. I will wait the ten years and reintroduce myself, I hope she remembers me.

CHAPTER 12

'THE DOUBLE STANDARDS'

Three months before we broke up the last time, I entered into a trade with a friend of a friend, we will call him Drunk. He was about six feet tall, dark short hair, very loud, pushy and annoying. In the trade I received a forty year old electric riding lawn mower. It was built by General Electric and it runs off of six golf cart batteries. The instant I heard about it, I knew that this was an opportunity to start a new company that would give me more time off, a good living, and it would be good for the environment. It would also give me the ability in the next couple years to start a new online company that I have been working on for over two and a half years, which will change the online dating industry.

After waiting for over two months to pick up the tractor, I forced the situation, it was a Tuesday. I had been on the highway to his place by half past ten that morning; he lived about ten kilometres out of town. I got there and he was working on a car in his driveway. I pulled down the driveway and behind the car. He was under the hood of the car, when I walked up to him, he said his buddy and he pointed to one of the guys on the other side of the car, just blew the engine in his truck and needed to get this car going for him as soon as possible. The guy said no rush, he could just spend the night and we could go do our thing. No, this car was a rare sports car and we wanted it running so he could drive it before he sold it, so he blew the comment off and kept working on the car. This was my forth trip out there to go get my side of the trade but he was a drunk and very unreliable. The problem was the tractor and stuff I was supposed to get were twenty five kilometres on the other side of the city. So I had to go get him, turn around, and go back through the city and out the other side.

I stood there for about forty five minutes and they said they needed beer. I ended up driving one of the guys to the nearest town, four kilometres away and back just to shut them up and get them back to work. When we got back, it took about another half an hour to get the car almost running. Then it turns out they have to go to the city to get tires, no point in sticking around. It was around noon, he says he needs about two hours to get it done. We all left his place at the same time, I went back home and picked up the trailer and went to Subject X's, it was about half past noon when I got there. I sat there all afternoon waiting for the Drunk to call. I found out the sun set at eight that night, so I had to be on the road by six to make sure there was enough light. Partner showed up and agreed to come with me to get the tractor. Crosser had been there for a bit before we left also. She had a little extra pot and Partner bought a little bit, then we headed out. It was just before six when we left and this time I brought the trailer, we didn't have enough time to stop back on the way through to get it.

On our way out of town, we tried to smoke a small pipe of marijuana but we were talking so much about the tractor and making plans we didn't finish before we got there. They were still working on the car when we got there. We could tell they were drunk. We pulled up and got out. He said he was just finishing up, it took about ten minutes and the car started. Then he had to go for a drive.

He lived on an acreage and was speeding back and forth in front of us. He told his buddy to hop in and they took off. We were standing in front of the house; the driveway was straight in front of the house all the way to the road, about three long blocks. When they got to the corner it sure looked like he was going to hit the ditch but he made a right and headed toward the highway. He disappeared over the hill, about forty five seconds later; they came back over the hill and passed the driveway. They headed the other way and kept going, we lost sight of them.

The drunk's sister came out of the house and asked where he was, we said he went for a drive. She was pissed saying it wasn't his car, he better not wreck it. What a nice guy leaving us waiting, things like that. They were gone for about fifteen minutes, then they came back, we were so pissed off for all the screwing around. When he parked the car, his friend and him grabbed a beer and started to talk, they would not get in to my car.

I asked Partner if he would pack a bowl to get these guys in the car, he said yes. I went to them and said if we got into the car we could smoke a bowl but he said he wasn't getting into the car until he was high and wanted more in the car. We said this was all we had take it or leave it, we smoked it then the four of us finally got into the car and left. On the way out to the tractor the drunk tried to pick two fights with me, he tried to pick a fight over me asking for my lighter back, he actually hit me from the back seat, just being a prick. I had to keep my cool; I had a plan for that tractor for the future and was planning to spend the evening with my girl. With a family there are certain things you must put up with to get the job done but I was close to getting really mad at the guy.

We had to drive back through the city and out the other side. We got to the field about quarter after seven. We disconnected the trailer and weaved the car into the tractor to pull it out; the four of us could not move it by hand. We attached a tow rope and I had to take a run at it to get it to move. It was hard on the car, the tractor had two flat tires and still had the snow blower attached so it was very heavy.

I was a little overly cautious when pulling it out, so Drunk, who by now could hardly walk straight, insisted on getting in the car and he hammered on my poor car and jerked the tractor hard core. We had to put four tires under the hitch on the trailer to raise it up so the back end was touching the ground. Once the tractor reached the trailer we had to put the car in front of the trailer, hooked the tow rope to it, ran it over the front of the trailer, which was pointed at about forty degree angle upwards, down the trailer and attached it to the tractor.

The drunk got in the car and just hammered on it. He did this for about fifteen minutes. The tractor finally was on the trailer, when I went and disconnect the tow rope, he took off in the car, floored it to the end of the field, pulled the emergency brake, put the car sideways and came back spinning the tires, I was so pissed. However I had to keep my cool, a little longer I will be curled up with her, I just needed this over with and the tractor in my possession. We finally got all the accessories loaded and strapped, got everyone back in the car after some work. We hit the highway, I had to turn around and go back for my tool set. I took it out to try to disconnect the snow-blower. Once I got the tools it was about quarter to nine and it was dark.

Once we were back on the highway, I was so pissed off over the sequence of events, the yelling, the smell of beer, the bagging of my car and just the rudeness of Drunk. I called Subject X and the Crosser answered the phone, she said Subject X was in the washroom. I said to let her know we were finally on our way back and should be there soon. Crosser said no problem and that was that.

When we got back to town, Partner said he couldn't possibly take any more the two drunks in the back seat and wasn't coming with me to drop them off. We went to Subject X's and I dropped the trailer, fast. I had to get back on the road before they tried to get into the house. They needed a washroom but I really didn't want them in the house, so I was taking them around to the alley but they jumped out at the corner and pissed by the neighbour's car, I was just getting more frustrated. Finally I got them home and out of the car, turned around immediately and headed back.

I was so looking forward to having some time with my honey; it was the only reason I was able to keep my cool all day with this guy. Knowing that the sooner I got it done, the sooner I could hold her and be with her. I got back to her place at ten. Partner and Crosser were still there, when I walked in to the house they were in the computer room and the opening credits were just starting for a movie they were about to watch. I was starving, I hadn't eaten all day but I stayed and visited.

It was a short movie and ended at eleven. Partner had to go and I needed help to unload the trailer at home. So we got up to leave and I asked her what her plan was, she blew me off again and said she didn't feel like it, so I said to call if she wanted a visit. Crosser stayed and kept her company. We had planned to spend the night before together, but she invited Crosser over and promised we would spend tonight alone and together.

We went to my place and Partner helped me unhook and push the trailer into its place, then he left. I was so angry that I got cancelled on for running late; she never called to see what was up and when I would be back. I wasn't out getting drunk with my friends, playing video games at a friend's for hours; I was just out doing what had to be done.

The next day I went by, about twenty to five. I was on my way to work so stopped to have a quick visit and drop off a pick that we used to pry the tractor off the ground. She wasn't home; it kind of bothered me because she knew I always stopped by before work. I left the tools to the left of the front door and went to work, it was Wednesday.

On Friday, she called me when I was at work and asked why I didn't stop by in the last couple days. I said I had and she wasn't home and I was angry over being cancelled on again. I told her exactly what happened that day we got the tractor and she said I was just out getting high with my friends. Those were her exact words, I instantly got angry, and I had to walk out of the restaurant, to continue talking. I said you are so full of shit!! She hung up on me, she knew if she hung up on me I wouldn't call her back, she knows from previous talks, many times, that I think that is the rudest thing you can do in the middle of a conversation, and she didn't like it either. We agreed the last time never to just hang up, to say we will continue this later, or something to end the conversation in a civil way, but able to continue at a future time.

She sent me a message on a social network about four days later saying thanks for dropping off the pick and hoped life was treating me good. That burned me to the core; I couldn't believe she actually dumped me over this, that she was that self centered and self righteous. I was heartbroken that the woman who said she loved me could be this self absorbed.

A couple days later I couldn't take it anymore, I had to see her, hear her voice, see her face, and look into those eyes. I called and asked if we could set up a meeting, I tried to set it up for the next day while Spunky was at school at my garage where we wouldn't be disturbed. She said she didn't have the gas, I knew she had a ton of pop bottles, I bought the pop. I said take some bottles in, she said no, if we were going to talk at my garage, I had to wait until her check came in to put gas in her car next week. She said that she was a welfare mom and she couldn't afford to be driving around, I should come to her. I said I always do, if she wanted to meet at the garage where we will not be disturbed it was her choice. She said fine but it would have to wait the week until she got her check.

When she got there I was leaning over the tractor fiddling with some wires. She sat across from me. It didn't take long for the conversation to make it to the day we got the tractor and why she is still cancelling on me. Then I said if she wasn't in the computer room so much we would have more time for each other and her house would be cleaner, I am not going to work all day and have to sit in the computer room until Spunky goes to bed. Then she said all her friends think I had been mooching off her for the last six months and they all asked her why she puts up with it. I never mooched off of her and she knew it.

She said I was always angry when I came over and her friends always knew it. Well come on, if you are with someone but never able to be with them because they would rather hang out with friends, wouldn't you get angry? Before you know it, it is just an auto response every time and if you are never alone, well then you're always angry. I kind of saw it while we were together but ignored it because she said she wanted change. In the end she asked me what is the difference if we sit in the living room or in the computer room to watch a movie? I said on the couch we get human contact, we can curl up and enjoy each other's company but she would only curl up to me in the bedroom.

LANDLORD ISSUES

In the summer of 2008 I was in the process of looking for a place to live, I was living in my motor home. It wasn't road worthy yet and the campgrounds were too expensive on a monthly basis. I found a place just outside of town that I could store some cars and my boat. I asked Subject X if I could move the motor home into the backyard so I would have a place to go when the house was over whelming and a place to sleep. At this time Spunky was sleeping with her most of the nights in her bed. It didn't mean I wouldn't sleep in the house once in a while but the house was so full and her bed was still in the dining room. All we needed was a baby monitor and I still had the wireless camera system also. I told her it would also give us a place to go when Kiddo was home to watch Spunky, so we could have alone time and she would make rent money. She said no boyfriend of hers was going to sleep outside in a motor home instead of in the house with her. If her house wasn't good enough for me, then I should go park somewhere else.

I have sleeping issues, I wear ear plugs, she always had a big problem with that for some reason, even doctors say it is a good idea if that is what it takes to get sleep. I always have been a light sleeper. I have always used garbage bags and duct tape to seal my windows from light. I have worked nights since the day I turned eighteen. She wouldn't even consider blocking same of the light for me a little at this time; she did a year later though.

I had been in my house for four years and living in the motor home in the driveway for over a year. I had told the landlord that I had my brother available to take over the house that way there was no need to look for a new tenant. They said it was ok. The landlord showed up on July second and told us that they were hiking the rent by fifty percent at the end of the month and if we didn't like it, to get out. I knew there was something up when they called for a meeting so I had a camera with me and got the whole thing on video. They went downtown and had all of our utilities disconnected. We used rain water for the toilet and candles for light.

One night when I was at Subject X's, I got a call at midnight from my brother, he had just gotten home and the house was broken into. I raced home and found my dog gone and the bathroom window ripped off. I called the cops, they said the landlord had called them and said they had no idea how to reach me and hadn't heard from me in weeks. The cops went to the house with them and allowed them to enter the property anyway necessary. First the cops had to check the house and that means the pound had to come get the dog. They said they went with what the landlord and said there was nothing I could do about it.

On September eighth, my brother calls me and says the cops and landlord are at the house and looking for me, he left and wasn't going back, he had warrants. I raced to the house, parked half a block away and walked up. The cops were rude and the landlord was standing behind them smiling. He had a possession order against the property.

Apparently the sheriff had put up an eviction notice on the door a couple weeks earlier, we never got it. The only explanation is the landlord took it down as soon as the sheriff left because we never saw it. If I had seen it I would have made that court date and shown the video. It was way past that point. I had tried to pay the rent but because it was only four hundred dollars, they wouldn't accept it.

When we were served, my birthday was two days away. My license expires on that day and I have twenty five hundred dollars in tickets against me. I just lost everything I owned except the shirt on my back and the dog was in the pound again. I did have a settlement coming in the next week for a car accident; the check was worth twenty five hundred. I had to go rent a room from my mom, I had no other place to go, Subject X never offered to help and I was tired of asking. So when the check came in I gave fifteen hundred to a lawyer who saw the video and said we had a great case.

In the end the lawyer screwed me because he entered into a consent order that said we would pay all the back rent at four hundred dollars a month, three months worth. And we would get access to the property for thirty days to move out. I didn't want to do it

115

but the lawyer said if I didn't take the legal advice I was given, the courts would frown upon it. What did I know, the lawyer paid the twelve hundred dollars out of the money I gave him and then wanted more from me. In the end the lawyer tried to come after me for an additional fourteen hundred dollars a few months later.

We got the keys from the lawyer and headed straight to the house; I took a video and started it on the way to the house to show what we would find. A few days before we were served, Mechanic asked if we could store his stuff in the house for a couple weeks so he could move. My brother and I said sure no problem. Well when we got to the house, everything was destroyed; I had four cars and the motor home there. The station wagon I used for doing drywall with my brother and the sprint I used for deliveries. The sprint had a side and rear window smashed. All license plates were missing; the awning on the motor home was ripped off. The outside water was turned on and had flooded the whole yard, the house door was ajar and everything inside was destroyed. They ransacked everything. Tons of stuff missing out of the motor home.

In the end I calculated ten thousand dollars in missing or damaged stuff. I tried to take him to small claims court. I did my research and screwed myself. I talked to three different lawyers from three different agencies and by doing that no lawyer would talk to me again because they didn't want to give advice different from the others, bloody ridiculous. I spent three days in the law library, which was just mind boggling and went to court; looking back I see my mistake but live and learn. I did have a solid case, it was all on video, and I just went about it the wrong way. I could still do it from my understanding but I need to put the past where it belongs.

All this could've been avoided; all the crap I went through for that year and a half could've been avoided if Subject X just would've helped me. I lost everything I owned, my driver's license, two jobs, all my tools, the canoe, keys to all cars that were on property, coin collection and a lot of faith in the law and Subject X. However, since getting rid of the life sucking delivery service, my attitude had changed immensely. I was not angry all the time, my road rage was a small fraction of what it was, and I was more relaxed and more sociable. Once I tried and failed in the civil court system the first time, I figured it was better to put it behind me then hold onto the thoughts of revenge.

GRANDMOTHER'S PASSING

Subject X had brought up several times how I am so rude to her parents. I never meant to be but like I said after a while you are just in that mood. Especially when she had days notice that her parents were coming for the night or weekend and never made time in the days before for us, alone. Many times I was pulling away, half a block away and her mom would show up and I would go back to help unload. She would tell me her folks would be here at a specific time and needed help to unload; I was there every time I was free. Always helped them with anything.

In our second last year together my grandmother died in Northern Alberta. My mom was running a delivery service and needed help with dispatching so she could go to the funeral. Subject X and I were talking but not together and our communication was breaking down. I tried to reach out again and again told mom she should call Subject X and see, she could use the money, little money but money is money. Mom did and got a hold of her and she said sure no problem.

When it came down to the last couple of days before mom had to leave, Subject X stopped responding to my mom's inquiries about dispatching, and she just disappeared and left my mom in a really bad position. She had to leave the company in the care of my youngest sister. That was a bad idea. Not even six hours after mom left, my sister closed the company at about six in the evening because she was mad.

I was working with my brother at the time doing drywall. I had to take over the company that night and stop working with my brother. Subject X left us in such a bad spot, especially me. So I had to give up my paying job for a week to run the company. I wasn't eating or sleeping and was working over fourteen hours a day. On the second day, I was so drained and tired that when I was getting off the couch I threw out my back. I couldn't move. I was stuck on the couch for the rest of the week. At night I went to bed but a couple of times my brother had to help me out of bed because I couldn't get up on my own. And I couldn't go back to work for a while afterward. It was very stressful on my mom, all because Subject X broke her promise, again, without so much as an email.

SPUNKY AND BEAR

My second oldest sister, number four from oldest to youngest, we will call her Prego and her boy friend Cook. Prego at this time is pregnant, about three months. She is five feet nine inches tall, dark hair about four inches past her shoulders. Cook is about the same height, about one hundred and sixty pounds with short, straight, dark hair. They bought a house and last fall they were rebuilding the fence around the yard. Subject X, Spunky and I went up to help. The day before, I had a friend do some welding on my jeep and I got a serious case of welders flash. I could barely see on the drive over and spent the whole day on the couch with my eyes closed and an eye mask to block out light. I went outside once in a while to see how things were going but the sun light was brutal on my eyes. One time when I went outside, I had just missed an incident with Bear and Spunky. According to witnesses and Bear, Spunky was in the way while they were trying to screw the fence down and was running in and out of the boards; she almost got hit a few times.

After about twenty minutes of people making it very clear that she was getting in the way, Subject X still did nothing. Bear had the drill in one hand and with his other and lifted Spunky up by the arm and moved her over behind him. She had bent her knees and wouldn't put them back down so she could be set down. He let go of her and she hit the ground. About six inches between her knees and the ground when he warned her for the last time he was going to let go. He did and she went and hid under a chair for a couple minutes. I came out a couple minutes later and Spunky was running and jumping all around like nothing happened, as a child does.

I found out about it a little later that day when we were done the fence. The version I got was different and a little more violent. When I heard it, I confronted Bear, aggressively. Bear is a brown belt in tiger claw kung-fu, well he was. It has been years since he studied but he is still plenty fast, you don't just forget that training. I walked into the living room and just laid into him. First time in twenty years I would have even considered doing something like this. Not only does he have the training but he is one hundred pounds heavier than me. I was prepared to be laid out if that was what it came to. I was angry and yelling; my mom came into the room behind me and listened. He didn't feel he had done anything wrong, I just kept going, I was angry. In the end the conversation didn't end well, I ended up back at Subject X's. And she started digging into me, hard. It wasn't my fault, I went and did and said what I could.

This was within a month or so of us all being baptized, so he went to talk to our minister. That night he apologized, he didn't mean to be rough with her, he was just focused on the job at hand. Spunky is truly one in a million, she knows right from wrong, she just has limited or no boundaries in most cases. She is the most out spoken child I have ever met, it is remarkable what comes out of her mouth but she must be taught limits.

I told Subject X to go talk to Bear and express herself. She finally did, he apologized and Spunky loves him. When they came over, she always ran to bear and demanded a hug; she was always trying to hang out with him. They came over four or five times after that and Spunky still ran into the living room and gave him a hug and talked to him, then all of a sudden Subject X doesn't want to bring her child there because of it.

In the five years I knew her, we never once had a romantic evening at her place, she never once came to spend the night with me, and she only took Spunky to the park when someone else went with her but not me. She never put me ahead of her friends and never meant a word she said about wanting me in her family's future.

The last time we got back together, we agreed to go and get counselling to help our relationship. At that time she wanted me to promise never to up and leave her again, she wanted a committed relationship, and we would talk our issues out like adults. I promised never to do it again. I assumed she was making the same promise, my mistake. During the three months of counselling, there were many times that I wanted to leave but I didn't, I had made a promise.

CHAPTER 13

'THAT NIGHT'

I was working that Saturday night and had passed her place a few times and noticed everything was kind of dark but her car was there. I couldn't take it, was she curling up to someone else already? It wasn't even a month since she dumped me and we were talking once in a while, why would she talk to me if she was seeing someone else? I parked the car a block away, pulled my hoodie over my head and walked toward her place. I walked past the front of her house; I see no signs of life. I go around the block and up the alley and in through the back gate. I walk up to the house and look into the windows, most lights are off, computer is dark and nobody sitting anywhere.

Ok, maybe her friend B.M. took her to her mom's. No, it is something else. I can feel it, my mind starts to race, my heart starts to beat faster, suddenly sweating like a pig and reality sets in. Oh my god, she promised she never to do this to me, she said she loved me and wanted me to marry her. Hold on, she could just be out. No way! I walked back to my car and went back to work. After work, I drove by and everything was the same, I knew she was with someone else. I went and grabbed the vacuum and accessories, parked in the alley just up from her place, walked in the yard and put the vacuum on the back porch then I turned around and left.

The next day I drove by again, it looked exactly the same. I had to work that Sunday night and I knew it was going to be hell but I drove by her place after the supper rush, there was a black ford quarter ton extended cab parked in front of her car, looks like her friend from Saskatchewan was down visiting. I headed back to work, got half way there and realized that truck had no roof rack, it was smaller also. I had to find out. When I was caught up at work I went by again, it was a different truck. I parked up the block, headed down her street with my hoodie pulled over my head. A couple more steps and I can see into the computer room . . . Oh my God! She is sitting there making out with some guy! My heart instantly started pounding harder than ever in my life, I wanted to die right there, I want to knock on the door, when it opens, kill them both, wait, I can't kill her she has a daughter that I care too much about to grow up with no mom.

I kept walking, went around house and picked up the vacuum off the back porch. I got back to my car, got in and screamed at the top of my lungs. How could she do this? End everything because I was late? I want revenge; I want her to physically feel my emotional pain. That is not possible, if I killed her she would not get to experience it, maybe a couple of seconds, which is not enough, it must be slow. Take her eye sight for life? Break her back so she can't walk for the rest of her life? I don't care as long as she lives in pain and with the memory of what she did to me. Spunky is home, I can't do it tonight, but he is another story.

I go home and sent her a nasty message, calling her a slut, wishing her all the pain in the world; she had slept with two roommates a while back while we were broken up, on the same weekend as far as I know. So I had to mention it, of course, I was so angry. I told her I had picked up the vacuum and she could pay for the stupid thing herself. It was a nasty email. I headed back to work to cash out so I could go back and wait.

It is now half past ten at night; I am back parked in the same spot. I get out pull up the hoodie and go around the block. I'm coming up to her house again. They are still sitting there making out, holding each other. Blood boiling, heart pounding, I want to knock on the door and give the surprise of a lifetime, wait find out where he lives. I get back to the car, light a smoke, I want to cry but I am in such a rage I want to see both of them in physical pain. I wait for another twenty minutes, time for a walk around again, coming up to the house again; he has his hand around the back of her neck. She is rubbing it as if to scratch her head, ok now I am madder, pissed off, irate, frustrated, crushed, all I see is red, and I want blood. Keep walking, don't give yourself away. At the car, I light another smoke and sit on the grass on the boulevard. I try to calm myself down but it doesn't work, my mind is picking up speed, I can't stop it. I finished my smoke, time to check house.

I walk in through the back gate and sit by a large log by her tent trailer, using the trailer for cover from the house. I sneak up to the back porch, look into the daughters' room, she's not there. I go up the side of the house to look into the living room, no kid on the couch and no lights on in Subject X's bedroom, where is the kid? I walk back to the log and wait; it is about half past eleven.

I sit and wait in the back yard, ok they are now standing at the front door, hugging, kissing, caressing, and I am in no way thinking straight. I can see straight through the kitchen window to the front door and there they stand, holding each other. I walked back to the car and got ready. Ten minutes and nothing. I get out and walk back up the alley to the yard, still standing there kissing. The front door opens, I run for the car. I am parked west of her intersection; he comes to the corner and goes east one block to the set of lights on the main drag, makes a right. I start the car, lights come on and I pin it to the intersection and turn south, I pin it to the next intersection and turn east and slow right down. He pops out on the main drag, I am still headed south, I get to intersection and turn south behind him. He made the next turn headed east again on a side street. What! He lives in the neighbourhood! How long has this been going on? How long has she been hiding this? I just can't stop my mind sometimes.

I continue to the next intersection and turned left headed east. I stepped on it a little and made the next left headed north, I got to the first intersection and instinctively made a right headed east. Sure enough there he was, making a right to the next main road. I just came from there; it is a main road, why is he turning there? Ok, he turns and goes to the avenue, I get to the intersection a little slowly to see which way he is turning, and he turns left. I head straight through the intersection and up to the next making a right to head to the avenue. There he goes, I give a little room and then get to the intersection and go left. I know there is a set of lights up there so I can't give him too much room. I make my left and head up; he is in the left lane which means he is headed straight through the intersection. The light is red and I drive a little slow as not to pull up beside him at the light. At this point I am sure I have already been made, those zig zaging turns were not needed, unless he thought he was being followed. We were doing the speed limit, I am about half a kilometre behind him, and I start to think he is playing with me. The road comes to an end and he turns right, I follow. This is now a road that runs along the north side and half of the south side of the city, he heads south.

He gets into the left lane, I stay in the right. We follow the road until the last set of lights on the south side. He takes a left and heads east, towards the boarder; I follow but think I have pushed my luck, so I pass him after the highway goes to one hundred kilometres an hour. I put about three quarters of a kilometre between us. I didn't expect to be heading out of town; I was kind of low on fuel. I must do something soon, slow down to ninety five. He is creeping up on me, I can't think straight, my heart is pounding, a surge of adrenaline like I have never felt before in my life.

The voice is saying things like, you can't use your car. You will be one of the first suspects; damage to the car will take a couple days to fix, not prepared for this. Bumper on truck is high and car is low even if you drop a gear and pin it, a P.I.T. manoeuvre is tricky, can't miss! You miss he will call cops, must work first time, make it count. Steel a truck and do it in the next couple weekends, he obviously lives out of town. Buy two identical trucks, insure one, and hide the other. When ready to proceed, switch trucks and plate, hit him hard, wreck truck, leave little evidence, finish him. Go hide truck for a year, dismantle it, expose of it and put plate back on original. A lot more was running through my head but in that last few seconds, I couldn't process, I was just so angry.

Here he comes, I am doing ninety on the highway out of town and there is a truck passing me on the left. My knuckles are white I am gripping the stirring wheel so tight. My heart is pounding, palms are getting sweaty, and I'm starting to sweat in anticipation. I hear this low voice, 'Don't do it!', and other things. Can't really hear it, sounds like a muffled scream for help. His front bumper just got beside my back bumper, just a couple more seconds and it should work and mess him up. Ok he is beside me get ready, the baseball bat is on the passenger side floor and seat belt is on, ready for impact in 3 . . . 2 . . . 1. GO!

Something stopped me; I was almost in black out mode for a few seconds. Part of me was looking forward to the whole thing, the adrenaline felt good. Although I was aware and am aware of the consequences, I just didn't care at that exact moment. We had traveled about twenty kilometres. I had to go back to town; I was almost out of fuel. Once he was about two kilometres ahead of me I turned around and headed back. It was a very emotional drive back. My mind was bouncing off seeing them holding each other. I went home. I was just so hurt and irate; I put it aside and called her. She answered and I said hello, I would like to come over and smoke a joint and talk, it was about quarter after midnight. She said she just got out of the bath and was going to bed. I lied not to make her uncomfortable and said I drove by to talk to her after work and saw her with her new man, I asked her how she could spend a weekend with her new man and not 1 day with me?

She said she liked guy's spending money on her and not expecting sex in return and they had spent over three hundred dollars on dates and she didn't sleep with any of them and she liked it. Then she said she wasn't expecting to meet anyone, she said they had gone out once or twice before. Well at this point it hadn't been a month since she ended it, which means they have been seeing each other for a couple weeks. She dumped me and moved on so fast, how are people so heartless? At the end of the call we agreed to meet at Tim Horton's by her place.

Right there I knew she had made a choice, she never asked to meet in a public place before, or anywhere for that matter. I spent over five hundred dollars month just visiting her. I brought Pepsi over every day; on working days it was one bottle at night, on days off it was two bottles. At work I get a free small pizza per shift, for five dollars I can get a medium. I always got a medium and shared it with her, five days a week. I always bought a ten dollar bag of marijuana minimal everyday and smoked it with her at night when we were alone. Then there were the chocolate cravings, the chip cravings and the cookie cravings.

On my days off I pitched in on dinners that were planned and I was invited to. The meeting at Tim Horton's went as expected, she denied any wrong doing. She says she was so pissed off about that nasty email that we were not good together, never on the same page and it was good that it was over. Again I asked her how she could make time for someone else but not me. She just deflected, I wanted her to change, I wanted this, and I wanted that. I said all I wanted was some alone time, a better quality of life, a living room I can sit back and relax in after work and a woman who keeps her word. If she wasn't in the computer room all the time things would have been so different, she deflected and said I was trying to change her.

I said if she wasn't always in the computer room, her house would be cleaner; there was always stuff all over the place. The conversation was getting heated and I said everyone I know has wondered how a woman who has all day can have such a messy house, what she doesn't know is that most of her friends have said the same thing at one time or another over the last few years. She got right mad and said all her friends thought I was mooching off her for the last few months, she knew what that would do, and the conversation ended. I always pulled my weight and then some, she didn't. I walked away, she asked if I was going to make the vacuum payment, I said I had not decided, she said she was calling the cops, I said go ahead and walked out.

I wanted to go back in and tell her I love her and would do anything to end this but how do I do that when she never wanted to be with me in the first place? The life you planned was all for nothing, the talks, the counselling, the family counselling. What every plan we made together was a lie. We have sent a few emails back and forth; they are in the next chapter to show what drove me to write this book

CHAPTER 14

'LAST EMAILS'

This chapter is all about the last letter and emails that were sent back and forth. These are included to show why I was so angry, frustrated and pissed off enough to even write this book. To the edgy of insanity. The emails start after our meeting at the coffee shop.

Email one from Subject X

> I understand your hurt . . . but realistically . . . we arnt good together . . . we are never ever on the same page in our conversations . . . after 4 years you still barley give Spunky the time of day . . . the only time you have talked nice to her is since councelling . . . so for 3 years you walked in and picked a fight with her . . . wheres the real relationship . . . bonding . . . i am doing these changes because of councelling . . . the group councelling has really opened my mind to the reasons my relationships self destruct . . . and the biggest is because i pick men from broken families . . . and exspect them to be family orientated . . . i am going forward in life because the stress and walking on eggshells because i never no what the new rules are . . . had to stop . . . 'RAJE' your a great guy and you will make someone very happy one day . . . but your right i should never have chased a guy who didnt want kids . . . it makes things hard . . . you are a great mind . . . but like i said all along if you spend all your time worried about the future you loose the moments in the now . . . .

Email two from Subject X

i am not doing this to hurt you . . . i am doing this so i can move forward in life . . . and i am tired of not being good enough . . . like the counceller said you cant go into a relationship exspecting to change the one your with . . . if the person your with isnt how you want them then they are not the one for you . . . i obviously do many things that you dont like and you have made them very nown . . . and because i cant or wont change it makes you angry . . . i am who i am . . . i am not purfect but i am me . . . and during the last 4 years i still am unable to please you . . . so like i said i am doing none of this to hurt you . . . even thou i know it does. i am sorry for that . . . it was not the motivation . . . i hope you can continue councelling and may the next person your withl be up to your standards . . . i wish you the best future and hope one of your buissness ideas takes you where you want . . . and thank you for saying your going to still continue your promise of paying for your vaccum . . . take care . . .

This was a letter that was dropped off with the vacuum payment for the month of June 2011, it was hand delivered by me in the middle of May. She was sitting in the computer room and saw me drop it off and walk away.

Dearest SUBJECT X

Here is the cash for vacuum. I am sorry for being so irrate in that message that night, but seeing you being so intimate with someone else was way to much. That was supposed to be me, we were supposed to get married, have a life together, travel the world when things turned around financially, help people all over the world, we made plans on many diffrent levels, was it all a lie? To say we weren't on the same level isn't true. You said you wanted all those things i did, what happened to those talks? I will be able to give that lucky lady the world, I thought that was you, guess not. For you to say ' . . . the group councelling has really opened my mind to the reasons my relationships self destruct . . . and the biggest is because i pick men from broken families . . . and exspect them to be family orientated . . . . 'is really heartless and mean, my mom should have stayed with my dad? Does that mean you should have stayed with dale? Is Danno doomed with her kids and family? What about SPUNKY, her parents aren't together and her father would rather be in jail then with her. Only a woman can over come the way they were raised? Do they? Doesn't being raised like that give me a better perspective of values? The first 2 years you said you wanted a man who was close to his mom, and I was, you said you loved that part, and know you say this? After the way I was raised and never laying a hand on a woman, what does that say? For you to say '. . . . after 4 years you still barley give SPUNKY the time of day . . . the only time you have talked nice to her is since councelling . . .' so for 3 years you walked in and picked a fight with her . . . 'that is really heartless and mean. 2 years ago you said SPUNKY missed me so much that she said if she started swearing would I come back . . . and you think there is no relationship there? You were always in the room, I did stop and talk to SPUNKY on my way past her a lot more then you think or saw. You make all the changes for YOUR family now, but when it was supposed to be OUR family it wasn't worth trying? How does that sound, I wasn't worth your time, wasn't worth the effort, but you sure wanted me to do this or that, name 1 time I failed you? Or didn't help? Didn't do what I said I would? Do you think if you made those changes I wouldn't have made changes to do more, I wanted to, just never any time. All I wanted was a better life style, more fulfilling and pasionate, why didn't you? Are you the only one that needed to feel needed?

When I said I loved you the last 5 times you got right pissy, but i do love you with all my heart, we had big plans for the future, and I accepted the responsibility, but it was all a lie on your part, I see that now, you eather were not ready and couldn't admit it, or lied.

And although you and I can not be friends again . . . I cannt see you with someone else, I was going to marry you, it was supposed to be me holding you, kissing you, caressing you. I would not hold that against SPUNKY. When you are ready I would like to see her, not to keep an open line of comunication for us, but because wheather you see it or not SPUNKY and I do have a wicked relationship, and i did accept her as mine, and she did call me her future step dad, many times, and she was happy about it, that's not a exelent relationship? I had to block you on facebook cause I cann't handle seeing your face and knowing I will never touch it again, but if you are willing to let me and SPUNKY spend some time at the park for her and me to spend time together, that would be nice, I have no problem seeing you in that few mins, it would be a fair trade off to see SPUNKY once in a while, but not for a while, still to fresh for her I am sure, but it is your call. I spent more time in her life then her own father, and it is not her fault, she shouldn't be punished. For this I will set 'US' aside, for SPUNKY's sake.

Wheather you want to face it or not you have convincided your self of all this stuff because it is easier to do then face the facts, YOU HAVE AN ADDICTION, it is easier to ignore, and gives the honey moon mood just to drop it and find someone new. If I was so wrong about those little changes, why have you done some of them? You seriously can't see how diffrent things would be? You cant see how all my plans in the last year were for OUR family? You dont see how those changes would have made such a diffrence in our relationship? I know you, if you don't yet one day you will, you will have to be honest with yourself sooner or later. I did try to get you out every 2 weeks but you just wouldn't make plans with me, but the past is the past and I am moving on like you, I do love you with all my heart and always will, that is why this hurts so much, the thought of someone else with you will haunt me for a long, long time, but that was your choice to end it and move on, now so will I. I will make the payments on the vacuum and please don't respond when I do, I really can't handle it, it was supposed to be me. Like I said as much as it hurts, good bye. I have never givin my WORD on this so now you have my WORD as who I am, I will NEVER bother you guys again. All future money will be in a envelope in mail box at night or mailed. All questions are retorical, do not need answers to them, already got them. There is so much more I want to say, but I don't think it would do any good . . . .

Good bye my love . . . .

THIS WAS SENT BY ME IN AN EMAIL AFTER A TALK WITH MY PARTNER ABOUT A WEEK LATER;

As hard as it is to think about, I wish you luck in the future. Well I have to do this after the talk I had with Partner last night and there are some things that need to be said at this point. Not picking a fight, but you ripped my heart out after all our talks. First it is not fair that you think our relationship had to end because we were stuck in ruts, face it or not it wasnt me. I was always trying something new, trying to plan a future. The changes you have made in your life were all my idea to save our relationship, you made it clear during counselling, even before that you were worried I would be the one to just walk out. We had plans for the future, we planned to get married, for you to make all these changes and think it was me holding you back isn't fair, it was the computer. All the studies out there say the computer is more addictive then crack cocaine, maybe one day you will see that it was the problem, all I wanted was 1 day a week to spend with you, really that was to much? You need to face the cold hard facts here 'subject x, I really tried to get you out, the fact that you were able to move on weeks after dumping me kinda shows you never really had future plans with me, or it is easier to move on then do what you expected from me.

I understand it is over, you ended it to date someone else, plain and simple, wheather you see it know or not, it was just easier for you. It was easier to just end it then take the

131

responsibility for the one thing that was the root of all our problems, the computer room. To think that I had togo so you could break your cycle is not fair after the life commitments we were supposed to have made. I did accept you guys into my life, but you wouldn't accept me. You know see how much that room was the problem? Then how come you cannt simpley face the fact that it was your addiction that caused these issues, you are right when I came over and there was always some one there I did get pissy, but that was because I just wanted to spend alone time with you, what was wrong with that, it wasnt me holding us back.

What would have happened if you made these changes during the counselling? They were changes you had to make, now that you have made these changes you still cant see the love I musta had to stick around and wait for you to snap out of it, then when you do, you feel I have togo because of our issues, our issues were a result of that room. I have had to start seeing 'the counsler' again because I am so destroyed that you could just drop me . . . . like you said, like a sack of pototoes is how you felt when I did it, so I changed, and you turned into what you said I was. I loved you with all my heart and everything I have done in the last while WAS to plan a future with you, maybe one day you will see it and take responsibilty with yourself, but you were not fair with your demands then behaving diffrently in your actions.

Face it or not, we were good together till you let your addiction control everything. All my anger was a result of that room, if I was frustreated when I stopped by and inavertently was rude to people it was because I was actually angery with you for not making time for us, the counselling said we had to make time, and I did. We were supposed to get married and be together for ever, that is why I am in such termoil, I was the one that didnt want to get involved with someone with kids, and know me and Spunky do have a good relationship it is over cause you refused to accept responsibilty and do what you expected from me. Why dont you see the big picture, this isn't my fault, if we had more time together do you think we would be here? If we had more time together do you think I would have been so frustrated when I came over?

You say it was about the sex, is haveing sex and expressing yourself once a week with the person you say you love and want to spend your life with really to much? That is only having sex 4 times a month, you think all your married friends, or friends that are in relationships only spend time together 1 a week? I am in such hell because you could be so cold after everything, ya, my messages were cold and hurtful, but not till I saw you 2 together, do you really think you were fair? I have so much more I want to right, but I know you would rather just move on, so I have already said to much, but I was planning a future for us and you bailed on it. You should consider talking to waylon or another consellor before you destroy some one else, and figure yourself out. It was very cold of you to just start dating someone else and throw it in my face about how much money these guys spent on you, I couldn't get you out of the puter room, how was I supposed to get you out of the house? I am just having such issues with the fact that after all our talking, planning it was easier for you to push me to the side and go with some one else, even if you guys havent had sex, I couldn't get you out of the house or alone for 1 day, but you can go on dates and make time for someone new, that hurts emensely, and again we seperate and you make all these changes that would have helped us so much.

So good bye, this is what you seem to want and I will have to find away to move on. As hard as it is to have to deal with the real reason why you ended it, I will obviousity have to sort it out. I will keep my promise on the vaccum, no matter how I feel deep down. We probably will never be friends again, I cant deal with seeing you with some one else, we were supposed to be together for ever, and wheather you want to face it or not, you got scarred of the commitment pushed me away and backed out. If we had time together I wouldn't have been so frustrated all the time. But I am stopping here, cause as much as I don't want to face the cold hard truth, we are done, and you have moved on. I love you Subject X, maybe one day you will see just how much I did and tried.

Good bye . . .

This was written before I started this book, I sent her a copy one day before her birthday. It was more a personal reflection at the time it was written, but I sent it to her any way.

This is going to take a while to write, so it is going to jump around. Maybe I will try to write a book, maybe its a diary, maybe its a tool to teach me, I am not sure why I am doing this, I do not know if it will help, but i must get it out. I am in my own personal hell, it is my own fault, I should have walked away that day after her birthday when she came into the backyard, I loved her more then life, I gave her the 2 things that I swore I would never give another woman, and in this order, my heart and infinite patience. Next time I will not have patients for someone to change, the next one will be more mature. the hardest part is, all the talks we had in the first year about wanting to change, She said she wanted more meaning in her life, she said she wanted to quit smoking, I offered to pay for the prescription for 1.5 years, was I not worth it? The last time we broke up, everyone thought I was trying to force her to quit, BUT SHE SAID SHE WANTED TO! How was I the bad guy again? Everytime I hear a car with an exhaust leak, I listen to see if it is an auto or a manual, if it is an auto, part of me hopes its her surprising me with a visit to really open up and talk. But I know that is not the reality, and it was all based on a lie. I will probably let CROSSER read this at some point, she is the only one that seems to be able to talk to SUBJECT X and get her to have any sense. If there is anything in here that might help CROSSER get through to T, even though we do not have a future together, and can not be friends again, it will help her in her next relationship, and more importantly, it should help SPUNKY. I can not beleive I will not be able to see SPUNKY grow on a day to day basis, I wanted to teach her to ride a 2 wheeler this summer, take her fishing, this is why I didn't want to get involved with someone who had kids. Time is moving so slowly, it was been 2 weeks today since I saw them together, it feels like a lifetime. Even if they have not had sex yet, she is able to make time for someone else, but not 1 day for me. Why did she think she was always the victim? Where did this victim mentality come from? She has to much baggage from past relationships and refuses to look at and change it, she demanded it from me though.

IN THE BEGINNING

Up to this point we had known each other 10-11 months. We were good together and had fun together. We also broke up during the next 4 years many times and always for the same reason, except one time, She would not make time for us. That was the root of everything, she never—had a romantic dinner for us,—showed up at my place to spend time 'together',—called out of the blue to say she wanted to talk and come to me,—got up and met me at the door when showing up to give a hug and kiss,—came to the park with just me and SPUNKY,—tried to get morning nookie,—and she never truly opened up to me. Can she name 1 thing I didn't do or at least tried once. I remember seeing her for the first time, although I knew she had a boyfriend, we had spoken 4-5 times on the phone, when I saw that smile say hello and those eyes so wide, I knew we would hook up, By the time I kissed her for the first time on her birthday, even though its hard to admit, I was already in love with her, I just didn't know it. I have never gotten so much pleasure from just a kiss, Even though the sex was one sided, scarce and repetitive, I never got so much pleasure from kissing and being with someone before. I keep thinking I should leave a rose on her car Thursday morning, but I gave her my word I would not bother her again so I don't cause problems with her new relationship, or confuse SPUNKY anymore then she is.

I got kicked out of bed several times in the first 2-3 years cause SPUNKY crawled in with us, I slept on the couch or in SPUNKY's bed, it was very hard on my back.

THE FIRST YEAR

It was GREAT, neither of us wanted to get married, we had fun hiding it from everyone, she sat on my lap when no one was around, tried to kiss me when she could, I would grab her ass when she passed by. Then I ended it on her birthday, even though I gave her 2 months warning I that was getting frustrated, and several times between, I should not have done it that day, but I was so angry I didn't realize it was her birthday.

But she came into the backyard and we reconciled, She wanted to make us public, HER RULE CHANGE ONE. I agreed. I got closer to the kids, how could you not, I spent ALOT of time over there, over 60% of my time, but not even 10% of that was spent with SUBJECT X. I also had brought NEAT to SUBJECT X's around the 6-7 month, and was rather rude about it, but she was still friends with her ex, I had to sit there and listen to them and she spent so much time with her friends. I guess I wanted to make her jealous, I wanted to spend the time with her, but even from the beginning she wasn't getting home until after 2-4 am every day.

THE SECOND YEARISH

I tried to get her to go for canoe rides, but she sat at home with her friends. I tried to arrange, get togethers in T's back yard, big fire pit, she wasn't interested. The second year I got closer to Spunky and tried to be Kiddo's friend. But nothing changed on her end, she was still out all night, 6-7 days a week at D and T's, She gets the computer and problems with D and T started. She started to have nights at home until 4am on the computer. Still not making time for 'US'. Tensions take a massive hike, how can you have a good relationship when you only spend 1-2 days a week for years?

THE THIRD YEARISH

We had broken up in the second year, we got back together because Spunky asked Subject X if she started to swear, would I come back and wash her mouth out with soap? That's a hell of a thing for a kid to say and accept. What kind of relationship must we have, that after over 4 months she would like to be punished by me, for doing something she knows will get her in trouble, just to see me. Subject X said that was her eye opener about Spunky's and my relationship.

I tried to get her to go for bike rides, but she can't sit on normal seats because of her back, I have had bout 2 dozen car accidents, sitting in the computer room on those kitchen chairs was brutal, but I got shit when sat in living room regularly, or went home to relax, that's unfair.

She suddenly wants to get married, and makes a very big deal about wanting to be with someone who wants to get married. I had to do some serious thinking, she said I was my own person and wasn't like my dad, I make the choices not to repeat the way I was raised, she was right then, but the BS she said at the end was the most hurtful thing she could have said, or ever did say. Its all B.S. to convince herself its my fault and not take responsibility for this. She said she wanted to give me a child, we talked alot about it. She said I wasn't understanding when she was working last year, she hasn't had any time for me over the last 3 years with my jobs, she never took time out of her time when I was working, she never did anything on my days off.

THE FOURTH YEARISH

In this last year, damn where to start. Now she says she doesn't want children. I tried to get her to go for walks. Subject X and I got baptised in the fourth month. I tried to set up a date night twice, once on Saturday nights, once on Mondays. 6 months ago we agreed to finally go to counselling, of her choice. It changed nothing. She spent all her time on the computer anyways. She says Crosser went from hard drugs to pot, and is still acting like an addict, she just changed one addiction for another. But so did Subject X. In the first year, Subject X had a small gambling issue . . . vlt's. I watched SPUNKY a few times so she could go put money into the machines, sometimes she said she was going to greens, but came back a little later. But once she got her computer, she stopped her gambling and moved onto the facebook and let it consume her. Especially once D, T and Subject X stopped talking. Then she always had Crosser over, it was not Crosser's fault, she called and asked, always. Then B.M. comes by 2-4 times a week and says shes NOT leaving until she has to pick up her daughter which was usually between 9-11pm. That got to me, all she had to do was so no I am spending the evening with my man, but she wouldn't and the one time that I am late, she gives me serious attitude and dumps me, then she tried to bring up all this other shit to convince herself that she isn't an addict or this isn't her fault. I can only take blame for the things that are my fault, which I have and a couple of them I had to do some serious thinking, soul searching and changing of my attitude, to be productive in a family setting but I wanted to do it for them and I did. But she wouldn't do it for me, she said she loved me, I saw the end before it began, why didn't I listen? I worked 3 winter months in a car with no heat, that needed to be boosted every time to get it started, the driver's side window had to stay down while I was out of car and I had a fan mounted to the dash to keep windows defrosted, IT WAS A COLD 3 MONTHS!!! I put myself through hell to pay bills, but all she did was complain.

She said she understood why we had to quit smoking and toking, to have a longer life together, a healthier life and the money we would save could do so much. 6 months ago we talked about traveling once we quit, it was what we both wanted, so she said.

I really do love her and Spunky with everything I've got, there is nothing more I can do to show her, she must show me, or she never did, she was kissing someone not even 2 weeks ago. She has moved on, I was going to give her so much, actually I already had, if that wasn't good enough then she doesn't deserve to be around when I am doing good in life, but it is hard to realize it is actually over. I devoted myself to her, she didn't. It was all a lie, everything she said was a lie. It burns me to my core that someone else is holding her, looking into those eyes, damn its hard to deal with. I sent a nasty message, the night I saw them together, I was so irate, angry, frustrated, pissed, flabbergasted, it still haunts me having those pictures in my head but I had a right to be angry, I can't get one day alone with her a week, someone she said she loved, and she KNOWS loved her. She said no one ever kissed her like I did, touched and caressed her like I did, she said I knew her body better then she did, it is easier to think everything was a lie then to face it that half was a lie . . . . which half?

THE LAST 5 MONTHS

When we got back together this last time, in 1 month I took Subject X and Spunky to dinner and golf, took SUBJECT X out to CoCo's and a movie, we went for a walk at the river bottom, I tried to do more, I suggested we make Saturday nights for us, the Saturdays SPUNKY was with RELAED we go out, on the Saturdays she was home, we spent the day together burning SPUNKY out so we could curl up but in that month nothing changed on her end, still no time for us and the counseling started. She said she didn't like the 1 week out on me, and 1 week at home, it felt like it was keeping track of who's turn it was???? Thats life, SPUNKY was only gone once every 2 weeks, you have to work with what you've got but again I gave and did, she didn't.

Although the counselling was my idea a year earlier, we went to a program she chose, she thought it would help, she said she would try, but she didn't. She says she showed me how much she cares by letting me be apart of her family, what about me willing to take the responsibility of her mortgage, bills and pay to raise a child that isn't mine, that means nothing?

COUNSELLING

The name of the course was 'SUPPORTING FATHERS INVOLVMENT', or something like that but when Subject X found out it was more about FAMILY'S not FATHERS, things went down hill, she thought with the word 'FATHER' it was there to teach me how to be a good dad, a father figure, and mate but it wasn't, it was about families working together as one on the same page, different paragraphs is ok, as long as you respect and support the others wants, needs and desires. They showed us how important alone time in a relationship is for good communication and human contact is needed no matter how old you are. During the counselling sessions, I had Mondays and Tuesdays off, I tried to set up another date night on Mondays, Spunky is in sparks so it was good time to go out or stay in alone . . . never once in 12 weeks did we do anything. B.M. makes time for her man when he is in town on days off, Crosser spends time with her man, why was I not worth Subject X's time? How do you let something go that was supposed to be beside you forever? I have taken her by the hand, looked into her eye's and laid my future plans for OUR family, she said she would love that life, its just so hard to imagine that its over.

STUPID VACUUM

If I was single, I had excellent credit, does she really think I would have bought that vacuum for myself? FOR $4000.00???!!! I had agreed to buy a vacuum, it was the best I had ever seen. I was living with Subject X, we said we were getting married, we said we had a future, to show her I was serious and was there for the long term, I bought one, 1-to show her that I was there for the long run, 2-she said she saw it before, she liked it and would like to have one. I wanted to show her that I would get her what she wanted, 3—it is the best and I wanted to show her that she was worth the best. BUT SHE SAW NOTHING!!!! Just like my bankruptcy, I am so glad it is done with, but I would have never done it with out SUBJECT X's worries. She said "I am worried that when we are married your old debts would put liens on my house." So I did what had to be done. I am sure it would have gotten done but not for a couple more years. I did it to show her that I would do what it took to be a good provider and she knows my future plans are huge. To top it off, I liked the vacuum so much I wanted to work for the company, I had to spend $100.00 on clothes, she threw it in my face many times about spending $100.00

on nice clothes for a job I lasted at for 3 weeks, WE SPENT $1100.00 A MONTH ON SMOKING AND TOKING!!! WHAT???!!!

She posted on Facebook that I was a con man and had conned her out of the vacuum and posted my name and she wonders why I want to just walk away from it. It was supposed to mean something to her, it was supposed to represent my devotion, my commitment AND I HATE LOOKING AT IT!!! But I guess when it took her 11 months to get the ring sized, how many guys would have had the patients for that? The ring she complained about for a year before, she wanted jewellery, funny everytime I gave her what she wanted she withdrew even more, she doesn't know what she wants and when she gets it, it means nothing, whether it is physical, sexual, emotional or a material object, exactly like Spunky.

THE DAY OF CHIN

She can't see how important that day was? Did she not see it would give her a full time job? Did she call me that evening to see how things were going? Or to see when I would be back? I was waiting for 2 months at this point to get that tractor, it was my last day off, Partner was supposed to invest, she couldn't see his frustration with me still not having the tractor so he could make up his mind? She thinks I would have rather been doing that BS instead of being with her, how is that possible? First she said I was just getting high with my friends in Chin, that is the reason she cancelled our evening and then broke it off 5 days later when I got angry. Then 2 weeks later she says it was because I ditched her to go hang out with my friends in Chin, then a week later I saw them together, and I had a right to be angry, she couldn't spend 1 day a week with me but can spend the entire weekend with her new man, who at this time she tells me they have been dating for a couple weeks and she likes guys spending money on her without expecting sex. But they were sitting there making out, intimacy is intimacy, how should I have felt? I started this new company for OUR future, Mon-Fri work, nights and weekends off, to spend time with her, I have already offered the whole company to Partner because I don't want to be here anymore, I hate SOUTHERN ALBERTA! I have given up so many shifts at work in the past 3 years, just to spend time with her but all we did was sit in the computer room, even on all my scheduled days off. She would go into the living room to watch movies when PARTNER brought his computer over but that was the only time. She did it so often, we broke up and got back together at that time, and I had to ask Partner if he had slept with her, she was spending that much time with him, so sad. The only other time was unless I brought pizza over after work and sat in the living room. She even tried a few times in 2-3 weeks to get me to start eating in the bedroom but that was worse for my back, thinking about it, everything I wanted, never really happened, in the end it was her way or no way. In the last year, I made drastic changes, fast and irrationally. BUT I was bottling it all up, when I look back and realize that I lost 2-3 things about myself, I am getting them back now. In the end as much as I want them to be apart of my life, I only have room for Kiddo and Spunky, I can not be friends with Subject X, I can't ever see me being ok with seeing her with some one else, she wanted someone to devote themselves to her, I did and she didn't do the smallest of things. How are you able to be friends with someone that you love? That said they loved you? That you agreed never to leave each other? How do you see them with someone else? EVER? How many couples only have sex 1 time a week, 4 times a month, taking out 'her' week. That is not a intimate or healthy relationship, and its my fault??? How do you show somebody what they mean to you, when they do not make time for you? Buy them jewellery? Spend hours/days/years sitting around waiting for alone time? Get close to the kids to show you're there for the long haul? Plan a secure financial future? Plan family days and couple's nights? I DID ALL THAT AND IT WASN'T ENOUGH FOR HER, what did she do? It must end, my heart can not take this yo-yoing with her anymore. Out of all 4 ideas for businesses I have worked on starting in the last 2 years, she has turned around and used each against me in conversations with her. She said she loved that part of me . . . another lie!? I put so much into my businesses and cars, because I am a passionate guy, does she think I wouldn't have put that into her? If she just did a little, I would have done much more, how is her time worth more then mine? The night of our $2.00 date, she said it was very romantic, imagine if I could get her alone for 48 hrs and could make plans that wouldn't get cancelled. After 5 years, the day I get something to build a new and brilliant company for the future, she leaves me, I just don't understand it.

SUMMARY

I wish there was some way to get through to her, so she could see how much I loved her, how much I tried, how the smallest of efforts on her part would have made such a difference. There is no such thing as fairy tales, in the real world you have to constantly work at something to make it better. At the end, all I wanted was 1 day a week alone, how is that too much? All of our issues can be narrowed done to 2 things, COMPUTER ADDICTION, and no TRUE COMMUNICATION FROM HER. It was all a lie, so she was not communicating. In the last 6 months in our 'discussions' I have asked her to name 1 thing that she did, changed and continued to do to help improve our relationship or future, she NEVER could give me 1 example, EVERY time, all she said was that her friends saw the changes, so I should see them, then she changed the subject, I have given her lots of things, I have done, but she can't give me 1 . . . It's good that it is over, she will never make the effort to come talk to me a 100% openly, deep down she has no courage, Her exact words to me 3 years ago while her and CROSSER were spatting and avoiding each other's phone calls were, "I would rather ignore a tough situation then deal with it, enough time goes by and things go back to normal." Not this time, and what kind of attitude is that? Wikipedia says "Courage (also bravery, fortitude, or intrepidity) is the ability to confront fear, pain, risk/danger, uncertainty, or intimidation. "Physical courage" is courage in the face of physical pain, hardship, death, or threat of death, while "moral courage" is the ability to act rightly in the face of popular opposition, shame, scandal, or discouragement." I have laid my heart, future financial plans, and future family plans I had with SUBJECT X, twice, she never truly opened up to me once. I thought we would be together forever, it is so hard to realize that I have to do come up with a new life plan, I spent the last 1.5 years doing what needed to be done to have a secure and supportive future with a family that wasn't mine and as it turns out it never was going to be. I can not live in a house where the 6 year old child has more freedom of speech, more rights, more run of the house. Because grandma pays for the satellite the tv, it belongs to Spunky ALL day and evening. When I did or said anything that upset, angered or caused any kind of fit, I was the bad guy. I do not blame Spunky, she is a child, she is supposed to push the boundaries, but it is the parent's job to set those boundaries. She gave me shit because I wanted to bring home some pizza for Bear for a couple months, I brought her pizza for years, my step dad, who has helped me out immensely over last 20 years, shared my basement suite and had no food, he was family, I just tried to help him and she gives me shit for helping family because it cut into her share, it also cut into mine, again, why was she so much more important then me. I can not live like this any more.

I helped her build, plant and weed her garden last year, cut here grass on company time, I helped do or get done her kitchen ceiling and walls, Spunky's room, her room, the bathroom, the outside of the house, I put a battery warmer in her car last year to make sure her car's remote starter would always work during the winter, I spent $300.00/ month going over and visiting her, I helped her with so much and all I wanted was some time alone, damn that was selfish of her!

I never got my balance from her that she promised for 3 years, we were supposed to do a liver cleanse 2 years ago, we even had a weekend planned, we were going to take Spunky to her moms for the weekend, but again she cancelled. She always cancelled.

Someone else gets to take her out for her birthday, gets to hold her, give her the birthday kiss, promise her a future filled with love. That is so hard, I gave her a birthday kiss that she said was the best kiss she had ever gotten. What happened to that girl I fell in love with, who wanted more meaning to her life? I didn't try to change her, she said she wanted to make those changes for herself, for our future, She lied, what other explanation is there? I got to close? Everytime I took a step forward, she stepped back, did she think I was lying and that I was just going to leave her? Doesn't she remember that I keep my word. But she is seeing someone else, I must live with it, move on, get over it, how? Am I wrong? Can anyone explain it to me in a logical way? Why wasn't I worth her time? WAS THIS MY FAULT?

IF SO, I NEED TO KNOW SO I DON'T SCREW UP MY NEXT RELATIONSHIP! Maybe I just need clarification, maybe I need someone to tell me I was not wrong, I just don't know anymore. She gave me crap for starting this grass cutting business, she said starting this business during the day AND working nights would leave no time for us . . . there was already no time for us, it was supposed to work so I could quit working nights as soon as the business picked up in a couple months. I told her this company was a stepping stone so I could get the online dating site up and running, she gave me shit again because I said that . . . ??? Because I wasn't satisfied with it and wanted more? Because I have drive, idea's, a sense to succeed and the will to make my dreams become a reality. She said she would love to do all those things to help people all over the world with the money from the dating site, now its a bad idea???? Should I stop building a larger net worth just because 1 succeeds, I should give up the others? Now that I see this written, it must be over, I have drive, why did I let a woman get to me like this? One day She will figure all this out, probably with Neat's help, one day. Subject X is far from stupid, just stubborn and lets her pride get in the way all the time. I just don't know how to let go, I guess that's how you know who was in love . . . who wasn't . . . or is it that I am so angry about being betrayed for taking care of business? WHY WAS I ALWAYS IN LAST PLACE WITH HER? Did she ever trust me? Even if she came and apologized and explained it all, I don't know if I could forgive her for ending it and moving on so fast. But that's not an issue, she has no courage. I am so torn up inside, I can't eat or sleep, I must do what ever it takes to unlock my head and body, it is time to lay the truth out there and let her go. The counselor said he can not help me any more, I am not allowed to go back to him to talk about this, he says I am locked in my head, I already have all the info, I just have to find a way to put it behind me. I have SO much more to say, I am constantly thinking of her, 24/7, but I need to stop typing and move on some how.

THIS IS THE LAST MESSAGE SHE HAS SENT ME AND HER RESPONSES TO THE ABOVE.

> 'RAJE' i appriciate your opinions . . . but we still differ on many of these issues . . . you see them one way and i see them

another . . . i hope you understand that i will never be what you want me to be . . . and i hope the girl your wityh next will have the patence and time to change the ways you want . . . may life be full of many wonderful things . . . take care

Because of this message I decided to write this book.

She contacted me one week before the end of june.

June 22 She sent—hi i understand that you might still be angry with me . . . and understandable . . . it wasnt an easy choice . . . but again we are at the time of the month where i get panicked about the vaccum payment . . . i understand that things are crazy but i do not have any money to cover the cost and need to know what your intentions are . . . please let me know asap . . . and i found the contract and there is still 3 years on it . . . i really dont think i can handle three years of worring every month and like you said its a purchased that you would never have made . . . maybe we might have to talk about returning it to the company and cancelling the contract . . . then neither one of us has the hastle of the vaccum . . .

June 23 I sent—What did I say about the vacuum? You want to worry about it, you go ahead, I am tired of repeating myself, it just proves you never trusted me or believed what I said. Now you say you understand that I have a right to be upset, go back and read your last 3 emails to me. You took everything in our world and flushed it because you didn't want to deal with a situation you created, you dumped me because I got mad, I had a right after what you did. If you came by to talk and I was sitting there making out with some one how would you have reacted? Tired of the hypocrisy, I wrote a 16 chapter book in under a month, it is just being edited by some friends, and if it is the last thing I do on the face of this planet I WILL get it published and let the truth come out. Think back what I said about that !@#$%& vacuum, figure it out. You made your choice based on previous relationships, thanks a lot.

June 23 I sent—By the way, the letter I dropped off with the last payment explained the plan on the vaccuum, reread it, I wasn't kidding. You send me ANY more messages inquiring about the vacuum in any way, for any reason I will make sure the payments are at least 1 week LATE!! Borrow the money from your new boyfriend or one of your good friends till I pay it, I don't care.

I AM NOT KIDDING, JUST 1 REFFERNCE TO THAT DAMN VACCUUM AND ALL PAYMENTS FOR NEXT 3 YEARS WILL BE AT LEAST 1 WEEK LATE, YOU HAVE MY WORD, TRY ME.

June 24 She sent—i just want to know about the vacuum . . . we were already broke up when i was kissing another guy . . . and if you do publish a book based on me i understand that i get royalties . . . so please due i could use some money . . . so again if i don't here from you by Monday with the payment i am cancelling it and letting the company know your address to collect the vacuum . . . have a great day

June 24 I sent—Screw you, I checked, you get no royalties, I warned you about contacting me about the vacuum again, this payment will be a week late.

This is when she went on the social net work and made a post on needing a lawyer to take legal action against me for the payments. I had only ever been late once.

June 24 I sent—I have always made the payment, all I want is for you to leave me alone, the payment will be on time, just stop messaging me about anything.

June 25 I sent—You want to use facebook like that to feel like a victum, ok, lets call child services to chat with Spunky about all the things she knows and see's about drugs. Then you can be a victim. You want to mess with someone, someone is going to mess with you.

July 4 She sent—just wanted to let you know that the trailer is cleaned out and is in the alley for you to pick up . . . i can give you about two weeks before the city stats to complain . . . so please com by and grab it when you can

July 5 I sent—Call the wreckers, wasn't kidding, no receipt, no next payment.

July 6 She sent—please give me the mailing address and i will give you the receipt . . . and since your the one with the metal buisness i thought i would give you the first dibs on the trailer . . . thanks for the permission to call the auto wreckers . . . have a great day

July 6 I sent—My mailing address

July 7 She sent—thank you . . . will send it and after every payment i will send a new receipt . . .

July 7 I sent—Fine, NOW DON'T CONTACT ME EVER AGAIN, this is what you wanted. You couldn't give me back any thing else, but you will try to give me back a trailer I paid you 2 years ago to get rid of, doesn't make any sense. You wanted me to leave you alone, SO LEAVE ME ALONE!! You didn't want to be with me, now I don't even want to know you.

July 13 She sent—i am going to give you your stuff . . . it has been sitting by the front door for all this time . . . was planning to drop it off when i drop off the receipt . . . i thought you might still want pictures of you and the kids . . . and your cars . . . if you still do then i can and will drop them off once the next payment on the 28 happens . . . or sooner if need be . . .

July 13 I sent—There is no next payment without the receipt for last month's payment, remember? If your actually going to drop stuff off I will unlock the hatch in my jeep and you can just put it in the back of it.

July 13 I also sent—Why do you keep contacting me over stupid, trivial bullshit? You KNOW you could have gotten rid of the trailer no questions asked. You KNOW I have only been late once in over a year with the vacuum payment. You KNOW you could have dropped my stuff off with the receipt on the front porch without sending me this last message. You know you said there was never a relationship between me and your family, and never would be. You know exactly how YOU ended it. You KNOW I said we can never be friends again, You KNOW you never wanted to be with me. SO THEN YOU KNOW THERE IS NOTHING LEFT FOR US ON ANY LEVEL OF COMMUNICATION. All I want is the receipt once a month, if you drop off other stuff just do it with no communication like I do. Every time I see a message from you I get more pissed with you, you expect me to respect your wishes but you can't respect mine and just stop. What the hell is wrong with you? I am finding it more difficult to keep these messages civil, STOP BUGGING ME!! You made your choice to end it the way you did. Live with it, and I will also. I am trying to move on with my life like you and don't need the past coming back to haunt me every couple weeks with dumbass messages about stupid shit. Just stop all messages, I am done being nice and doing things other peoples way, I am doing this my way, and that is telling you politely, do you really want me to start sending back nasty messages? JUST STOP! or I will start. I want to be left alone.

On July 21/11 she dropped off my stuff and the reciept from June 28/11 for July's payment, I sent her this message . . . .

July 21 I sent—I have talked to a lawyer and I have a right to have a copy of the contract. I will make next weeks payment and want a copy of the contract when you drop off or mail the next receipt. I was expecting a copy in the stuff you dropped off but you didn't include it. When I receive it I will make Septembers payment. Thanks again.

What really got me going and made me say the payment was going to be late was the fact that she insists that I give her royalties for this book . . . I have no intention of making that call to child services, but when you are going to go on the internet and cause problems for someone, put them down and insult them, shouldn't you think of their reaction? What lengths they might go to show they are actually the victim? How a person can only take so much before they come out swinging? Where did people's common sense go?

You look at her first 3 emails in this chapter from the middle of May, she wants to make sure I am going to pay the payments, its my vacuum she says. I make it very clear my intentions on the vacuum, and for her not to contact me again over it. Then again she does a 180 with her next emails at the end of June, and wants to return it. I have invested $1100.00 into it and I am supposed to just give it back. I think she contacted me for another reason she just used the vacuum as the topic to start a conversation. But the conversation didn't go the way she was hoping and now she is making herself out to be the victim. If she was only honest how things would have been different.

CHAPTER 15

'KEEPING TRACK OF MYSELF'

This chapter is more of a daily thought dumper. A place to hopefully see a change in myself over the course of writing this. At the start of this chapter, I am about a third of the way through writing this and I have only been typing for a week.

May 25/11—Tomorrow is her birthday. I had big plans for this weekend, to think that someone else is holding her, giving her a birthday kiss, promising her all the things she wants. It is eating me alive, every second of every day. I bought 2 roses, one for me, one for her. I brought mine home and I'm watching it die, hoping it takes this pain with it when it's dead. I dropped the other one off at her place, left it between the front doors; she will find it in the morning. I miss her but after seeing them together, I am irate, frustrated and just so pissed off at life, what a waste of 5 years.

May 28/11—It's Saturday night, she is with him celebrating, could have been last night, I can't stop, I need to know if they are together. Why? To know for sure means driving by, what would that accomplish? If he is not there would it help to see her alone? Not likely. I still am not eating or sleeping.

June 2/11—All I think about is them, every second of everyday; it is starting to really haunt me. But the last 48 have been brutal, I couldn't stop myself and I tried. Last night during work hours I drove by, only her car was there and the house was all lit up. I went back to work. The whole day was hard, my head was going nuts and I just couldn't turn it off. I miss watching movies with her.

After work I parked a block away, got out of the car, lit a smoke, pulled my hoodie over my head and started walking. My heart is racing, is it because after these bushes I might get to see the woman I love, or will seeing her make me more pissed? Crossing in front of the house I see no one, but all the lights are on. Walk past, still nothing. Walk around the corner and go up the alley, stop at her gate, what to do. I put my left hand on the fence and say "I love you Subject X, why did you do this?" I had to know; I opened the gate and walked in. I walked to the garden, watching the house to make sure I am not seen. Figures, it is the same as it was last fall.

I walk to the back porch; the patio has been painted white, nice, now it matches the house. I walk to the kitchen window. The bathroom light is on, the living room TV is on and a light in the living room is on somewhere. I walk around the corner and up to the bay window, peak in. There is my love. Sleeping in bed with her TV on. I can see her legs only, covered with a blanket, she is alone. So? She is sleeping on her left by the looks of it, weird; she usually sleeps on her back.

I peak in a little further, maybe I can see Spunky. Oh crap, too far and SPUNKY is sleeping on the couch, I miss her, OH NO! She is not sleeping! Her eyes are open a little watching TV. Tap on the glass and wave at her? No! Get out of here! From start to finish I was at window for about 3-4 seconds and left as soon as I had seen that she was awake.

I left, walking up the alley; I tried to figure out if it was worth it, yes. I have had the images of them together running through my head for over 2 weeks. These new images will give me something else to recall, how long will this work for? I must stay away. How, to me, they are still family. How can she look at herself in the mirror after doing this to me? How can she sleep? I am so pissed.

June 3 (Friday 2am)—Well today when I woke up, I could feel the weakness in me from only eating one piece of pizza last night and hardly eating in the last month. Thankfully I have access to cases of ensure, but real food makes such a difference when it goes down and fills that hole. I was shaking all afternoon, not sure if it was from malnutrition, or from going by her house last night. My mind has been racing since I woke up, before I opened my eyes, it's all consuming. HMM . . . just had a thought . . . am I in love with her? Or with the person she said she was????? I learned last week, she is telling people that in order for her to get out of the ruts in her life, I had to go, and our relationship was the rut. I have had a real problem wrapping my head around that one. But it shows that she lives in Denial. She never, ever actually said she was wrong, about anything. She said many times that I was right, I would predict something 1 week or 6 months before it happened and it would happen. I can see patterns in almost anything and rather quickly. I did see the patterns with Subject X but after our 'LIFE' talks in the beginning, I fell head over heels. Dumbass. We just got along SO well that first 10 months, she said she never dated anyone for so long without having one issue, neither had I.

June 4, 4pm—Today is not any better, shaking all day, I just keep going over it in my mind. I ate more yesterday then I have eaten in last 4 days, so it's not from lack of food, it's from the lack of something or someone else. I so badly want someone to go over there and talk to her, why? I know it wouldn't do any good, she will never say it was her fault, even if she could, she can't admit it while in a relationship, what would that make her? She would have to admit she was wrong, never going to happen. That is the reason she ended up with someone else so soon, she can't admit when she is wrong, she would rather throw it away then take responsibility for her actions. It's almost midnight, I am not able to stop my mind, and I want to drive by so badly. I drove by at 715pm, B.M. was there. Why did I do that? I could have avoided it easily, just cause his truck isn't there doesn't mean anything, B.M. could be watching Spunky and she is out on a date. Today has been very hard, I almost smoked an entire pack of smokes already, at this rate I will have smoked a pack and a half today, that is odd, I usually only smoke one pack a day.

June 5—Just woke up, I realize how bored I have been lately, the depression is trying to take over, I must try to change that this week. I keep thinking about how I spent so much time over at her place in the last 5 years, that I have no other place to really go hang out,

I guess this is loneliness. We used to watch one movie a night, that's a lot of movies over 4 years. The last couple weeks, the TV has been playing a lot of them, all I have are memories, and I truly wish I could erase them. I wish I had never met her. It's Sunday night, she will be alone tonight, I so desperately want to go by later, but I know better. I hope. I must change my mind somehow. It's 1am, I think writing it down is starting help me see the big picture, there never was a future and I should have trusted my instincts, or at least after the first couple of incidents, paid attention, I will not be sucked in by another woman like that.

June 6—Ya the writing is helping, I am still thinking about it all the time, but I guess I am starting to accept it. That in its self kind of bothers me; it's just hard to accept. But as every day goes by, I am adding so much to the book and realizing I fell in love with someone who never existed. It was just a shadow on the wall. I hate all these father's day commercials; this is one of those holidays I was looking forward to, a card from Spunky. It is almost 1am, this is the worst time of day, my mind just thinks of them, and how I miss them.

June 7—This morning is a rough one, I had what I call a nightmare, I dreamed of them again, it wasn't a bad dream but any dream about them is brutal and I have to consider it a nightmare. All I want is to see them, all I do is think about them, I wish there was an actual way to describe how I feel deep down. I have gotten new info last week that is haunting me big time. I heard her and her new man are having issues already, something about a dead wife or girlfriend he can't get over it. He should count himself lucky, he can still visit her, she didn't leave him to be with someone else. He doesn't have to live with the fact that the woman he loves left him to be with someone else, is being touched by someone else. Here I go again; I must stop my mind from thinking of them.

The Crosser is supposed to be back at the end of this week. She is the one that can talk and get through to her. She is the one that always wanted to see us together. As much as I want her to try to fix this, it is not her responsibility. I have always avoided becoming better friends with her because I didn't want Subject X to think I was intruding on her friends. Maybe I should have tried harder, but it was so hard when she didn't want to be alone with me.

June 8—I weighed myself again today, still 15 lbs lighter then I was 1.5-2 months ago, crappy, I need to put that weight back on somehow. My head is racing, I keep thinking of them together, talking every night strengthening their relationship, leaving me buried in this mess. It literally haunts me on a minute to minute basis. Its 8:14pm I can't turn it off, I want to drive by, why? I know it will do no good, maybe tonight, why? To see them sleeping and know I will never be a part of their lives, today is hell. I was sure I heard her car last night, was hoping she was coming to talk, wait, it was 2am it won't be her. It is 10:09pm, I was sure that was her car, it's too late so I am not bothering to check the window. I must stop this way of thinking. Its now 3am, my mind is just racing, I need this book out of my head, I am about 2/3 done, it is helping me take my mind off of things for a bit, but my main thoughts are still of them and wanting to go by and see them. Even if they are sleeping, I hate her for doing this to me.

June 9—Tough night again, little sleep, can't seem to turn it off again, I need answers. Its midnight, I went by at 2:00pm, she wasn't home, must of been at work. I went by at 7:45 pm, she was home with B.M. I want to go by tonight and take a look, I have been thinking about it all night. Reading this over, I don't like the pattern.

June 10—Well I didn't go by last night, but I really wanted too. 11:22pm I am so angry, I can't turn it off, why did she do this to us? More so, to me. 1:07am, I miss going over there, I came so close to driving by after work, but it's Friday, it would be a mistake I am sure, but I can't stop thinking about it. I feel it stirring around, my '6th' sense kicked in about an hour ago. I have learned to trust it. I get the feeling something happened somewhere, not sure if it has to do with subject X directly or not, but I feel something. 3am I am getting really tired of these father day commercials. 3:43 am I just had a realization about the fishing on the mountain.

June 11—11:01am—It's Saturday morning, I have been tossing and turning for hours, the thought that someone else gets to wake up with them, see their faces in the morning, here I am, stuck looking into a mirror, into the eye's of a very angry man. Someone else gets to look at her as she opens her eye's in the morning, it burns me so deep inside. Today is going to be a bad day, what did I do to her, to deserve this from her. The weekends are the hardest to get through, knowing she is making time for him, to talk, hang out and be together, in the end, all I wanted was one day a week to spend with my love, what the hell is the matter with that @#$%^ woman?! 3:41pm—Great, another movie that Subject X and I watched countless times. 1:19 am—Another movie we watched together, I miss having her curl up to me and fall asleep.

June 12—7:12pm—The logical part of my brain is starting to come back, it never has come back this fast, my mind and heart must be moving passed it, that still sucks. It is still on my mind all the time, but I am starting to see her real colors from rereading of the chapters on her. 10:57pm—I want to drive by so bad, but I am able to control it better. The questions are still on my mind all the time, but I am starting to accept this.

June 13—3:26pm—Today my head is spinning again, all these damn father's day commercials everywhere, I wish there was a way to fast forward the next 3-6 months. Although it is getting easier, it is still painful. It still races through my head and I still get mad about it, not as much though. Now I get to start with a true woman, someone who will do what she says and promises, as I do. Someone who knows that a person's word is really all they have. I see light! This book is almost done, finally. I got it down to 16 chapters, it kind of feels good to have the truth down on paper, I am so tired of thinking about it, so tired of trying to explain it, soon it will be out there. 1:16am—I am done the book, except last chapter, the wrap up. It's hard to believe it is all over, the book and us. Time to finish the editing and get it ready to send it out to the publishers. It kind of feels like a weight has been lifted, but it will always haunt me.

June 14—8:45pm—I am doing the editing on the chapter with the emails, I am so pissed off. I can't believe the nerve of it all, the total denial, reading that chapter has set me back, and my mind is racing again. I am almost done this book, now I need someone to talk to. I need the Crosser, she was there for all of it, she is a good friend, I should have reached out years ago, and maybe we wouldn't be here. I guess I have been dreading the day I finish this book, but in reading it over I see the truth, I just don't understand it. 12:41am—It is no longer a question of why she broke it off, the question should have been and always will be from now on . . . why did she say she wanted all those things when she really didn't? Why did she lie? I must stop looking at the end betrayal and look at it from the beginning of the lie's. I just ignored it for the last 4 years; I should have walked away when she came back out of the house from helping Lincoln the day after her birthday.

June 15—7:57am—I woke up this morning thinking about it all, so damn mad. 9:23pm—another movie we used to watch over and over. 11:39pm—I had to go by her house, why can't I control this yet? Hard to tell if she was awake or not, didn't walk up, but I really want to go back. I started shaking when I got close to her house, I am still shaking, it is getting worse, my heart is racing and my mind is racing, please go away. 1:42am—I miss them so.

June 16—Again, I woke up thinking of them, when will this end? I need my peace of mind back. 9:44pm—I couldn't help it, I had to drive by, it is so hard to stay away, no calls, no emails, deep down I know it is for the best, but that doesn't make it any easier.

June 17—I just found a ton of pictures of Subject X on my phone, my god was it hard to see her face, I started to shake, my heart raced, I was sweating, I am so pissed off after seeing those pictures, I had to delete them. I kept all of the pictures of Spunky though. 3:08am—those pictures put me in a state of rage; it has been with me all day. I hung out with an ex for a couple hours tonight, even when she was sitting on my lap, nothing, I felt bad. Not guilt, but am finding it hard to be with anyone else, I just don't have the 'urge' anymore to be with someone, not even just for sex, what happened to me? My head is just racing; it is Friday night, are they together? Should I drive by, they will be in bed by now, ya, that is a good idea, what am I nuts? It would solve nothing and it has the potential to make me worse, how do I turn this off? How could this choice of hers, be better than us being together?

June 18—Wow, did seeing those pictures yesterday ever stir up some serious emotions in me, how do I get rid of it? How do I put this behind me and move forward? Father's day is tomorrow, that burns me up, but not as bad anymore. Without them, I feel useless. They say the right woman makes the man, if she wasn't that woman, then I am looking forward to meeting her and becoming what I can be. 10:04pm—I need Monday to get here so all this father's day stuff stops. 11:26pm—My head has just gone nuts since I had seen those pictures yesterday, I want answers, to questions, that will never be answered, it's hard to deal with. I miss having her cuddle up to me during a movie so much. 12:41am—It burns me that she would rather be with someone else, I want to drive by, but it's Saturday, he is probably there, or she is out there, awesome. 12:59am—I just ate a whole small pizza, I haven't been able to eat even half of one for 2 months, plus a can of soup and pack of crackers this afternoon, finally food. I could be getting laid right now and the thought of being with someone else is still disgusting, not her, but I never thought I would be with someone else, it almost feels like I am betraying her, how backwards is that, hey?

June 19—Again, I woke up and it is there, kicking me in the head, heart and stomach. I can feel the tears, but I can't let them out, it is father's day today, I guess in reality it doesn't matter what day it is, I have no children again. It is getting easier, but I still need and want answers. I can't believe I meant that little to her. I will hate her forever for doing this to me and for putting me in this state of mind. I need to find a way to bring some joy back into my life. 11:09am—It looks like I just sold another car, I have sold 3 vehicles in the last month, 1-turbo 300zx, 1-boat, 1-Buick regal, lost over $4000.00, whatever, time to get rid of all the old and start over. I still want to know why she threw away the best thing in both our lives. 9:16pm—I drove by 8:25pm, her car was there, but I couldn't tell if she was even home, I didn't really think it would help, I knew it wouldn't, so why can't I get control of it? When will I be able to control it? 10:44pm—I went by again at 10:21pm, I can't take this. I am just revved up right now. It's

Sunday, even after 2 months I still want to spend this time with her. I need father's day to go away. I need it all to go away.

June 20—I just saw her driving down 13th street, which has put me in a bad mood again; I just want to know, WHY?? 11:21pm—Well I am rather amazed, I did drive by twice today and even with seeing her this afternoon, I am doing ok, still on my mind every second, but it is getting easier, I think, it just sucks being alone and knowing she isn't.

June 21—I woke up 3 times last night in cold sweats; it is getting easier to see the big picture and just how selfish she really was. 9:56pm—I saw Subject X, Spunky and B.M. walking home from the store today and they saw me. That is so hard to see them, my first impulse was to jerk the wheel, but there were too many witnesses and I don't want to hurt Spunky. Just seeing her brings out the rage in a fraction of a second, I still want to hurt her, but I know it would accomplish nothing. 11:53—I went by at 11:15pm, what a bad time to try to quit smoking pot, I haven't had a hoot all day and there is nowhere to get it this late. My head is bouncing hard core, what do I do? How do I get her betrayal out of my head, I loved her! Why? This is the exact reason why I had to delete all emails and pictures; it is too hard to even see her name. What did I do to her, to deserve what she has done to me? It's been over 2 months, why am I still so wrapped up in this crap! I crave revenge! I need to get rid of this dark passenger somehow, HOW? I wish I had a friend to talk to, at this time it feels like I will be alone forever, but I still want her, why am I not getting any better? I want to drive my truck straight through her house. This passenger must go away somehow. Why does she think she is always the victim? Why does she think her crap doesn't stink? I will not give out her boss's number to people anymore; it is time to cut out all the selfish, self centered, inconsiderate people who stick their noses where it doesn't belong out of my life.

June 22—7:38AM—I have been up since 7:00am tossing and turning. Since seeing her yesterday, my head is just getting worse, after everything I did for her, after everything I have had to put up with from her and her friends, to get dumped the way I did, really makes me want to go across that line and cause immense physical pain to all of them, every single one that stuck their nose in our business, especially SUBJECT X for all her manipulation of her friends against me. 8:23am—I couldn't help it, my head is going completely insane right now, I drove by at 8:00am, why can't I stop this crap in my head? I am shaking big time in anger, I WANT REVENGE! I had such big plans for this summer, now I can barely get out of bed, what's the point? 3:36pm—I have smoked over half a pack of smokes already today, seeing her yesterday has really messed me up. 9:24pm—I feel rather good right now, odd I have been thinking of her all day. I can't wait until this is out of my system permanently. 12:10—weird . . . No hoot at all yesterday, I went all day until about 9:00pm, since I haven't been so relaxed, clear minded, not 'HIGH' and enjoying it. I have been thinking about it all evening, but from the angle I should be, everything she said she wanted, everything she said she was, was 1 of 3 things, 1-It was all a lie and she had manipulated me from the beginning, 2—She is lazy, self centered, hypocritical, or 3—She has an addiction. I feel the best I have in over a month and a half, I know it will be gone tomorrow, I know how my mind works. But it is odd that I am even having one good day this early, it has never happened before, it is nice to see.

June 23—1:58pm—I had to drive by just now, it is very hard to know she is home and I can't see her, this is what she wanted, I will do better without her, she was just keeping me down with her selfishness. 4:40pm—She sent me a message asking about the vacuum payment and whether it should just be returned because she doesn't want to stress over it at the end of every month for next 3 years of payments. After what I have gone through in the last 2 months, I will keep the vacuum and she can stress for the next 3 years, she deserves it. No matter how much stress she goes through in the next 3 years, it won't even be 10% of what I have gone through in the last 2 months. But I am in such a good mood knowing that it will get to her at the end of every month, for the next 3 years, as much as I want to not want revenge, stressing her out sounds awesome. I feel great, happy, and joyful; I hope she chokes on it! I know that is a harsh way to look at it, but after where my head has been for the last month since I had seen them together, I deserve a little peace of mind. 10:58pm—I am taking such solace in the fact that I get to control her stress for next

3 years, I feel GREAT! 11:56pm—I had to drive by after work, the house was completely dark, she must be out of town, there are always lights and a TV on, it has sent my mind racing a little but I have much more control now that I know I have some control over her emotions for once. 12:28pm—driving by was a mistake, my head is spinning, she is out there with him, I must stop doing this to myself!

June 24—12:56pm—It turns out she was probably home last night, I drove by twice already today and she was there, I need to stop putting myself through this, I must remember that it was all a lie. I feel rather good again, we have mutual friends that have told me she has gone all over the social network calling me a con man and asking for legal advice against me. There is a lot of bad mouthing going on there about me; maybe talking to a lawyer about defamation of character law suit is in the future. 1:17am—This whole thing with the vacuum has gotten way out of hand.

June 25—9:17am—Well I sent her a small email this morning because all the stuff on the social network. 10:33pm—I couldn't help it, I knew better, but I drove by, her car is gone, she is out of town with Spunky, with him. That is why I know not to drive by on the weekend. Tonight when I go to bed they will be together, my head just started racing, not as bad as usual, but it was bound to happen. It's really not fair that it is easier for a woman to find someone new, or maybe I just have more morals on some things in my old age. But I must look at the possibility that they are at a friend's and could come back later. It doesn't matter, either way the logical part of my brain keeps saying it and its right. A small part of my mind will not let her go, if she would only make a 100% effort and explain everything, I would try to help fix it, isn't that sad? The logical part of my brain says to have nothing to do with her, but I would ignore it just to try. Would I be able to keep my cool and get through it? I don't think I could. It is a no win situation, love is a feeling that needs to be eliminated. 1:14am—Funny thing, I reconnected with the girl that showed up that father's day 5 years ago, we are just friends, but she is having personal issues and with what I am going through I believe it would benefit both of us to have just a friend of the opposite sex to hang out with. It would be nice to have a friend again.

June 26—9:23pm—My head is spinning, how do I bury this love? It is Sunday, I want to call her and talk so badly, what do I do? I want to go by and see them tonight, this is why I didn't want to fall in love, I gave her my whole heart, how do I take it back? Why can't she just admit and explain what she did? It could change so much, even possibly fix it in time. Why do I still think like that? After her selfish greed this week, why do I still love her? I think at this rate, I will end up going by tonight when I know they are asleep, I want to see them so badly, I miss them, why? 12:09am—I was actually able to subdue myself, I did not go by like I wanted to, I still do, but I won't. I am so torn up, do I hate her or do I love her? Once again, a no win situation. I so badly want her to tell me why, but I already know why, she refuses to get over her past relationships and one of these three, 1)—Addiction, 2)—laziness, 3)—or she just lied about everything she said she wanted. How did I become the bad guy in all this?

June 28—2:01pm—Yesterday was a tough one, my Partner and I had a falling out and I am buying him out. It actually feels good to be the boss again. I dropped off the vacuum money at 1:30pm, with a small note saying the following . . .

"This is the last vacuum payment I am making until you mail me a receipt dated for today, June 28/11. It must also say that all payments are caught up, if not you can take me to court.

I feel better lately, I still think of them all the time, but the realization of it all is starting to settle in, I own my own company again, 100% mine. I still owe thousands on 3 bills, but know I make more money. I am still trying to edit the last half of the book myself, but I am finding it really difficult just to get through chapters 9-10, I am not looking forward to proofing any of it, I am sure it will bring it all up again, but it must be done to finish it and to refresh my memory as to why I can't try to contact her. She did this with her pride and greed, that is what it boils down to, but I still think about trying to fix it, I believe we were meant to be together, I also believe that there is more than one person for each of us. She didn't want to have a happy life with me, so I will find one of the others and get what she opened up inside of me, the good stuff.

June 30—Wow! There is a massive force trying to push me closer to my dark passenger. My partner stole all the company equipment two days ago after agreeing to be bought out, the police won't do anything, they say I have an excellent case for civil court and that is where this will go. I can't believe everything that has happened in the last 2.5 months, to push me down a path I am trying really hard to stay away from. How the hell did it come to this? How could I have lost everything in my life that meant anything to me over a stupid tractor? All I wanted and tried to accomplish was a better way of life? I am so irate inside over the turn of events that I am actually calm, my mind is racing so badly over everything that I can't stay focused on just one of the things that have gone so terribly wrong in the last couple months. Now I have to come up with a whole new life plan, I have nothing holding me here anymore, no family, no business, and no reason to stay. The time has come to get out of here, but where to? How? Time to formulate a plan and try something new, somewhere else. I have lost everything! All I have ever tried to do was the right thing, to build a future for me and the ones I loved, how did it come to this? Why did it come to this? Just to push me, just to see what it would take to push me over that edge? Maybe it is time to just go live beside a lake in the back of my truck, I just don't care anymore.

July 2/11—2:41am, Saturday night—She is still on my mind but with my partner stealing all the company equipment the other day, I am focused on that, a nice change. I am leaving town, I bought a large camping trailer, it needs work but it will be great. After everything, it really wasn't meant to be, I find that so hard to believe, but it is what it is and it was her choice to make. I can't wait to get my trailer at the end of the month.

July 3/11—Its Sunday, I have been dying to drive by all week, especially tonight. But I won't, soon enough and I will be out of the city so I am not tempted.

July 4—Last night was brutal, I had nightmare after nightmare about her, why?

July 5—I had nightmares again last night, why is this happening again? She sent me a message today asking to move a trailer of mine, I paid her $100 dollars 2.5 years ago to get rid of it, just another excuse for her to make contact, I told her to call the auto wreckers and get rid of it. As much as I want to, as much as my heart wants to and as hard as it is, I am sticking to the logical part of my brain and I am going to continue trying to burn that bridge, it must be over, it is what she wanted, so I will enforce it. My head is just racing, all day, I can't get her out of my head, it is starting to piss me off, I want to put her behind me, I guess I need to put them behind me. 10:31pm—It is taking everything I can do tonight not to drive by. I am just having a tough time today realizing I went from having a family, a business and plans for the coming years, down to losing everything and going to live in a trailer, funny. There is a reason I told her never to contact me again, just seeing her name in my inbox makes my heart race in anticipation for a split second, then it all comes back and gets me angry, I just want her to leave me alone so I can forget and get over her. All I want is a receipt once a month, like she expects the money, is that too much to ask?

July 6—I had nightmares again last night; I am getting really tired of this. She sent me another message saying she will send me a receipt and thanking me for giving her permission to get rid of the trailer, I gave her permission numerous times over the last few years, she is just doing it to try to open communication, I just keep trying to shut it down, why can't she just leave me alone? At this point I do believe she is trying to open communication but I keep shutting it down, I have to, I know she will never do the right thing. As much as I want to, I can't, I won't, but I think about it all day and apparently I have nightmares about it. But that will end at some point and I can't wait.

July 7—I had severe nightmares last night, I have been up since 6:30am, I need her to leave me alone. 10:26pm—My head has been racing all day, I didn't realize telling her to never contact me again and trying to burn that bridge would be so hard on me, but it is the right thing to do, I hope. 12:30am—It took over again, for the first time in a while I drove by, I couldn't stop myself. Her lights were all out and her car was there, that doesn't mean anything, but at least it is getting easier. Part of me still wants to be with them, but logically, it is time to let go of the best friend I ever had, I want a family that will never be mine; it is time to find my own.

July 15—She sent me another message yesterday saying she had the rest of my stuff and would drop it off with a receipt after the next payment. Again I am sure she did it just to try to open communication, but it is the wrong way for her to go about it, which means nothing has changed. As badly as I want to rebuild that bridge, I must continue to throw gas on it and burn it to the ground and I will. What it would take to try, she is not capable of that kind of patience, humility or openness and she has no courage to just lay it on the line.

July 21—She dropped off my stuff and a receipt this afternoon, 3.5 months later, I heard her car and when I went outside she was loading the stuff into my jeep. I stayed back until she was done and gone. Seeing her was so brutal, damn I miss her. I wish she would grow up and take responsibility for the sequence of events. This is all on her and her relationship issues. Why does she let her pride make her so stubborn? I never gave her any reason not to trust me. Damn I love her; I must get out of this city before I go insane. I drove by a little while ago, why am I still doing that? It just hurts every time I do, so why do I do it to myself? 12:20am—I finally ate something after work, I can't believe seeing her has sent me into such a whirlwind, I think I might have to resort to drastic measures to make money so I can get out of Alberta, NOW!!! I don't think I can wait until May 2012, or I need to resolve this with myself somehow. I want to keep writing, it has all come to the surface all over again. I have invested over $1100.00 into that vacuum; I must find a way to do this transaction on a monthly basis with no possibility of us crossing paths.

July 22 1:07am—It is Friday night, I just got off work. I want to drive by so badly, but that is such a bad idea. It has been haunting me big time all day, yesterday I brought everything to the front of my brain again. It is time to get another full time job and save the money I need it faster, I need out of here ASAP. If I left next week, it would not be soon enough.

July 24 9:49pm—My head has been racing since I saw her, it is Sunday, I HATE SUNDAYS!! I feel like a broken record for two reason's 1—I keep repeating myself in here, I am getting sick of it, 2—it keeps replaying in my head over and over, although it is slowly fading, it is still very loud. I still want to know why, but what does it matter now? Why is it still eating me alive? I have accomplished so much in the last 3 months, I am so tired of having to stay busy to keep my mind occupied to forget the betrayal, I want to be able to relax and truly enjoy life. I wonder if she is. I wonder if she is happy with the decision she made to end us. The answer scares me.

July 25 12:56pm—I had nightmares again last night; I can't stop thinking about it. I am not so sure I believe in love at first sight anymore. 2:04am—I just went for a walk to her place to drop off the payment, the window for the cats was open so I through it in so no one could steal it. My head has been racing again all day, I know I have months of this to go, I know the next woman I am with, I will marry. She would have to be a good friend first to get me over this, to reopen my eye's to love. But I will look for her, everywhere I can.

July 28 3:03am—I saw an old friend today; she grew up and got married, had a couple kids and is now filing for divorce. She was only 17 when I met her seven years ago. I gave her my number, she said she'd send me a text, I hope she does, it's time to find a new friend. As I have said, life goes on. It feels good at the possibility of finding someone new, someone who wants to spend time together. Even if she doesn't call, the feeling is still a good one. I have to start giving out my number more.

July 29 1:27am—M head has been spinning all day, not as bad as it used to so it is getting better. I want to talk to her to badly, I want her to tell me why she did this, I want to know why she couldn't spend one day a week with me, but can make time for her new man, it just doesn't make sense. But here I am repeating myself again, I loved her with all my heart, how do you let that go? I can see that it is getting easier, I can feel it getting easier, but it is still difficult. It is time to stop thinking about it and her and let it all go, but I have said that so many times in this journal it has almost lost all meaning.

July 30 3:05am—Another movie that we used to watch, I guess we watched a lot together. That's ok; I am starting to find the humour in it all. I mean that, it is funny that I ignored that voice in my head, funny that she ended it the way she did over her pride, funny that she brought out the tender side of me and doesn't get to experience what I am truly capable of, I believe I have hit the low point of our break up, now it is time to go up.

August 17 12:38pm—Yesterday was Spunky's birthday, I miss her, them, why? They aren't my family. Crosser came back a few weeks ago and I have been talking to her, it has helped me realize just how selfish and self-centered Subject X is and was. I still have nightmares all the time, I still want to be with her, but it has been about 5 months, so why can't I let it go. It still haunts me every minute of everyday, but not as bad or as much. I am looking for love again and will find it with a real woman, but it is hard to let go of the past when there was such possibilities. Missing another one of Spunky's birthdays just tears me up inside, but I am sure I will see her in 10 years or so when she is old enough to make her own decisions. Even if Subject X tried to be honest and explain herself and open up, I do not believe I could ever trust her again, so there is no fixing this, I just have to keep putting it in the past.

August 21 11:59pm—I have met a very nice lady online, only about an hour and a half away; I am going down to meet her in two days. My head has been racing all night. Part of me is angry because I have to go through this again, getting to know someone, tell her about my medical condition, put it all out there, but I can't keep it to myself, that wouldn't be fair.

CHAPTER 16

'WRAP UP'

Let me make this perfectly clear, I did not write this book for your pity. I don't want it, nor do I need or deserve it. Many people in this world have had and have it much worse than me, much worse. It is not written to get you angry, mad or frustrated with Subject X or anyone in her circle, they have the right to make their own decisions. Everything is just background to get to this point, this point where life must start over.

I am the guy, in the corner, quite, watching, figuring people out. I don't even have to hear the conversation; it is all in the face. I am shy until you get to know me. Then I will not shut up; maybe even offend you with my honesty, or sarcasm. Well I used to; I had to bury that for the last few years, no more. I used to always speak my mind; I haven't been able to do that for a long time. I miss it.

I am including the last messages that were sent back and forth between Subject X and I so that you can see why I have such a rage inside. After all I did, changed, accomplished, planned and dreamed about. All for our future together as a family, you need to see what drove me to write this book, even at great humility to myself.

I included a diary that shows how it haunts me on a daily basis so that you can see the change that happens over time, to see it does subdue, slowly and painfully. If it didn't, if it just disappeared, how would you know it was there. They say time heals all wounds, some wounds need more then time, but few people know what that is and very few of them have the courage to do it. Do you know what it is?

The first eight chapters have some very personal information and it is all true. I go into some very personal stuff to show you that I have nothing to hide, that by putting all that info out there and humiliating myself, I am not making stuff up or trying to humiliate Subject X, it is what happened, it was just the truth.

When the Gambler and I ended six and a half years ago and I went for mental help, I also went through a battery of tests for my health. While seeing the counsellor, he diagnosed me with OCD. He said I talked so much, he learnt more about me in one hour then he learns about others in months, I was very open, like this book is. When I told my family and friends they all said 'No kidding'. I was the only one that didn't see the OCD, but it explained a lot. It is why my mind would race all the time, I thought I had found the antidote, but in the end it was just napalm for the smouldering fire.

When going up or down stairs, there has to be an even number of stairs, when walking, if one foot steps on a crack then the other must also. The concrete pads that make up a sidewalk, even number of steps, per pair of slaps. I count stairs so next time I know if I have to miss one for the even number, little things like that. When I found out, I counted it as a blessing, I seriously over think things, maybe that's why I have been able to start so many businesses and have plans to start more. Maybe that's how I was able to write this book in under four weeks and wrote no less than five chapters at the same time, up to as many as ten.

I see the big picture from every angle, once in a while I miss one, but not often. I am able to put plans together and into action in an alarmingly fast rate. Some people have told me recently that I jump into things a little fast, they are right, I do. I see the possibilities and just go for it, time to slow down.

It is also a curse, I can't turn it off. I am very passionate in everything I do, when I give or put my heart into something or someone, I do it with everything I've got. But after a while you get tired of being the only one passionate about the present and planning a future. When someone goes out of their way to screw me over, hurt me or come after me, I take it very personally. How could you not? If you put all you have into someone or something and it fails due to no fault of your own, how far would you go to express yourself? Would you cross that line? Where is that line for you? Or is there even a line?

It feels like there is a monster inside, it just begs to be let loose, it tries so hard to get out, it was gone for so long, years, then in one night, one look, one act of betrayal, it was there, at the surface, in record time, in just a fraction of a second. It only wants to be released for a couple seconds. Just long enough to show how I truly feel, but the consequences would be devastating, for everyone involved. I must keep it caged; I must find a way to feed it without giving it what it wants, until it goes back into hibernation. Then I need to kill it, once and for all. How do you kill something that is a part of you?

I have this other feeling, a feeling I have only been able to show a few times in my life. And wouldn't you know it; it was in the last year. I do have a lot to give and want to give it to someone who deserves it. The couple times I showed it, I put a lot of thought and effort into it, once it cost me more in fuel driving around looking for what I wanted, then the whole evening cost me. She said it was the most romantic evening she had because of the thought put into it. Without fuel, I spent a dollar and a half. It was homework from counselling, spend no more than two dollars and have a date night. The next week was her turn, she never did do it.

I have lived all over western Canada, different groups of friends have said the same thing to me, I am very resourceful, you have heard the saying 'This guy could be dropped off in the middle of the forest and next morning be on your door step with a gun, breakfast, newspaper and clean shaven', I am the city version. Money isn't everything; there is usually two ways to do every job properly.

When working on one of my many cars, I am always thinking two or three steps ahead. When working on a business idea or plan, I am very thorough and focused and look at it from every angle. Sometimes I have let it consume me because it was a way to escape the frustration in my life at the time. And in order to be a business owner and be successful, you must be focused, and willing to make sacrifices for the greater good, there is always a bigger picture.

When I am planning something nice, it also consumes me, I want to do something different, something that will be remembered. Isn't that the point? I like to go out once in a while, but I like to do other things that most people wouldn't even think of.

I put my past were it belonged, in the past. I let go of all the anger, hatred and frustration I had towards woman, to be with a woman, who did nothing but live in the past. I did get jealous a few times, especially when we broke up, but that is the way she set it up. She never wanted to spend time with me, so of course I got jealous, when we broke up; I thought it was because she wanted someone else. If the person you are with doesn't make time for you and keeps cancelling your plans what would you think? What would anyone think?

The worst part of this whole thing is that I will never be able to see my child again. Ya, I have considered Spunky as mine for a while now and the fact is I can never see her again. Even if Subject X says yes, I hope I have the strength to say no. We can never get back together because she never wanted to be with me in the first place. We can't be friends because to see her with someone else will hurt too much. That means the only time I could see her is when her mother is single.

I will not bounce in and out of her life anymore and that is the hardest thing to deal with out of it all. She wanted me to build a relationship with Spunky and after three years she started to say she wanted me to be her step dad and she loved me, I said I would be her step dad and loved her very much. Subject X took it away for no real reason and said there was no relationship anyway, so goodbye. I will wait until she is old enough to decide for herself.

The second worst part of this is, she is telling people in order for her to get out of her ruts, I had to go. The fact that it was me holding her back, I tried so hard but all she did was sit around smoke pot and play on the computer over eighty percent of the time. Since we ended it, I have started a lawn care business, completely overhauled the online company I am trying to start, wrote most of this book, still work five nights a week doing deliveries. If anything, she was holding me back. I spent so much time sitting around waiting for her to spend just the smallest amount of time with me; I gave up on my stuff, just to be with her.

Since our break up things have really started to go my way. That kind of sucks because when this change in my life happened I was sure she would be by my side. Instead, the pivoting moment in my life, when things actually turned around, right to the day, she dumps me for doing what had to be done. As Partner said, she was just looking for a way out and the night I got the tractor she cancelled just to piss me off.

I went through hell for the couple days before I told Subject X about my condition. I really wasn't sure if I should, just friends was nice, but that is the risk you take when share that kind of information because you fell in love. Hard to believe it could be used against me so much when nobody knew about it, funny.

I am tired of always being the bad guy. When Subject X and I hooked up I told her to tell her friends it was me that was making her come home. Make me out to be the bad guy I said, I was used to it, whatever, so we can spend time together. Instead she made me the bad guy for all the wrong reasons. I am not the bad guy, I am the good guy, I was just mixed up with a bad girl, a lazy girl, a damaged girl that didn't want to get better.

As you can see I was a rather angry kid. I was not a nice older brother; I obviously had anger issues that turned into rage issues in my late teens and early twenties. It really manifested itself when I got my license on my eighteenth birthday. I started to drive fast and crazy from the beginning, it just got worse over time. The driving experience I got from all the delivery jobs taught me how to drive very well, I always have to make a spectacle of myself and was always doing something stupid behind the wheel. Except when I had kids in the car. I still do, I like to drive fast and the faster the better. And I am very good at it, to the point that I am looking into semi professional racing.

When I read that book when I was twenty or twenty three, I started to think I could take a life. I didn't think it would bother me, I still don't. So it was a matter of doing it and not getting caught. Look at where technology was twenty or forty years ago, where will it be in another twenty or forty years. There is no way I am going to jail, I decided a long time ago if it came down to it, it would be SBC, but the whole point was so it didn't come to that. I like my freedom and am not spending years in jail. At one of the lowest points of my life, just before I spent that month at the lake, I looked to God and realized that taking a life would be easy, getting away with it just takes planning, but how would I explain it standing in front of the pearly gates? How would I live with myself if I wanted to be a Christian? Or even a decent human being?

With taking a look at the state of the world, with all the evil in the world, there must be a devil, but you can't have one without the other, so I realized there must be a God. When I truly realized the scope of this at the age of twenty eight, I had to rethink a lot of stuff I had planned for my future. Would growing pot, blowing things up, creating false identities and ultimately taking a life be the way to live? It is very hard to change one's own thought pattern, it is hard to go from thinking a life isn't worth anything to thinking it is everything. Letting go of the past pain and betrayals is a very hard thing to do, to become a better person.

I have watched a lot of TV and always watch crime shows like all the CSI's, all the Law and Order's, criminal minds, real crime shows and my favourite, LIE TO ME. That show is awesome! I have learned a lot from these shows and even did some reading on the actual science behind LIE TO ME, it is neat. I have always been able to tell when someone is lying or holding back something, I have just ignored it for the last few years. A person should always go with their gut feeling, it is usually right. Instead society goes with the flow, people do the popular thing, and an individual gives in for their friends. If you are giving in, or can't speak your mind, are they really a friend?

That is why we live in North America, everyone has the right to do what they want, when they want, we have the right to believe in whatever we want. Like I said earlier in this book, just because you were raised a certain way, or it is the popular way to think or to do something, that doesn't make it right. All decisions you make will be judged in the end, how will you explain the wrong ones? If there is no God, then there is no devil, then where did all this evil come from? No God means no heaven, so what would it matter how you lived?

The key is to find that person that is true to you, do not settle. Being alone for an extra two, five, ten years is nothing compared to going through the pain of having it all fall apart after you give it your all. Do you want an angry relationship? One that frustrates angers and pushes you to limits that are so dangerous. Who does? The key is to stop and talk it out before it goes too far, to make compromises, commitments, to hear what the other is concerned about and take it seriously. Isn't that what love is?

Is there a difference between physical abuse and emotional abuse? Which is worse? Are they equal, just different results? If someone does this to you, makes you feel like that, is there any going back? Again, few people realize time doesn't heal all wounds, there is a second ingredient.

Maybe deep down I am a coward, maybe that is what stopped me that night. Maybe it is just wishful thinking, getting the ultimate revenge after being stomped on. Maybe thinking of it, obsessing about it, planning it, imagining it, is just my brains way of copping and how good it would make me feel.

Maybe it was the logical part of my brain, realistically, trying to pull the move I was going to would have done more damage to my car, making me the first suspect due to paint transfer. Maybe it was the realization of the set of headlights coming in the opposite direction, witnesses. I am not going to jail.

I truly do not know what stopped me that night but I am thankful it did. I will never put myself in a situation like that again, next time;

there won't be a next time. I learned my lesson really hard this time, but I did learn it. Don't go down a road were your gut tells you there is a dead end, no matter how strong you think your vehicle is, the further you go down that road the more speed you pick up, the dead end comes out of know where and it will crush you when you hit it.

So what is the point of this book? Some people are going to think it is for revenge, some will think it is to get the truth out, some will think it is for closure and maybe part of it is, but I wrote this to help people. I know there are others out there that have given all they got to another and been crushed by the hypocrisy. There are others out there that think the only way to express themselves is through violence towards their spouse. There are those out there that do hit women and unfortunately, some of them are killed by an abusive spouse. Like the first chapter says, we all have the choice, right or wrong, what is yours?

If an individual frustrates you to the point of even thinking of violence, is it worth staying with them? Is it worth being so frustrated all the time? When you touch your spouse in any way, it should be loving, never aggressive, no matter how good you think it will make you feel, no matter what they have done, your spouse doesn't deserve to be hit for any reason. The funny part, after everything that she did do and all the things she didn't do, I never, ever thought about hitting, harming or laying a hand on her until I saw her with someone else.

There is nothing wrong with going to see a counsellor, therapist, marriage counsellor or any agency that helps couples to communicate, or an individual grow. There are free counsellors everywhere, you just have to look. It could save one of your lives by stopping the frustration and opening communication. There is always another way, violence solves nothing, but it can sure feel good at the time, but most things that feel good, are not the right thing to do.

That is the point of the book, to show that a man can go through a lot, especially in relationships and still not hit a woman. I have gone through a lot in my past relationships and believe by sharing my past pains and betrayals it could help another to see that they are not alone. I know there are others out there that have gone through more, much more then I have, do you really want to be in that position? Who does? Love is not like that, obsession is.

She was the love of my life, all three of them were. It is time to let go, move on, find a woman that knows what she wants and has the courage to go for it, is honest, knows how to communicate, faithful, resolves conflict as it appears and believes in the golden rule. I can move on, I can let it go, I will let it go. Time for life to start over, time to put myself first and build something, tons of ideas and nothing holding me back. What's holding you back from just going for it?

EPILOGUE

Here I am at the beginning of November 2011, it's been six months, and sometimes it still feels like yesterday. Having to do this final piece is difficult. I stayed away from this book for the last couple months because it is still too fresh. And in the last week or so of working on it again, it has brought up a wide range of thoughts and emotions. Once published I don't think I will read the final product, ever!

I went to the doctor about two months ago and learned there is a cure for the hep-c, so he sent me for a ton of blood tests and an ECG. My blood work came back slightly better then expected, however the ECG results said something else. When the results came in I was shocked. It turns out there is an underlying medical issue I didn't know about, or even suspect. My whole life I have always felt drained, no energy, it was very hard to get out of bed, hard to get motivated. I always went to work, always worked at what had to be done but I always felt like the life had been sucked out of me most. Even after a good sleep and waking up feeling refreshed, I just always had to push myself to get up, no actual energy. It was really tough on nights I didn't sleep well; I usually spent most of the day in bed.

I thought it was possible depression; I didn't have a clue why I would be so depressed and just ignored it and worked through it. I didn't believe that I had a right to feel depressed and always figured that, if it doesn't kill you it makes you stronger, I was very wrong. I am lucky to be alive, again, but aren't we all? I came to terms with my mortality a while ago; we are all dying, just some faster than others. You have to make the best of the time that you have, you don't know when it will end. Bear has a saying, you never know when that airplane engine is going to fall from the sky and take you out.

I may have a heart problem, according to the doctor, on one end of the scale you have a normal person's heart rate, on the other end of the scale they call it PAST, meaning 'Half Past Dead', that is where my heart rate is. Just about half the rate of a normal individual. That means I am a V8 engine, with about four dead cylinders, I have to go in for a pacemaker by the looks of it, I am only thirty seven and it turns out that I needed it this whole time. It is the reason I have had such issues getting up after a bad night's sleep and why I am always cold. I always have to have a sweater close by.

Maybe it saved my life; if my heart is beating so slowly then maybe that is why I am in such good health after twelve years. The hep-c cure is supposed to work, when I am running on all cylinders and because I am in good health otherwise, the cure will have a better chance to work, or it's just my attempt at being positive.

This book goes to the publisher next week; I want it published in case I do have a complication with my recovery. If something does go wrong I want Spunky to one day have the option to know the truth, that I love her and didn't leave her of my own accord. I hate the fact that she thinks I don't love her, that I walked away. I didn't and will wait the 10 years to be a part of her life, if I am around. I have an abundance of patience for the ones I love.

So I am trying to get my affairs in order, get all my bills caught up, pay off some personal debts and tie up some loose ends. Odds are everything will work out fine, but the Boy Scout motto is 'BE PREPARED', yes I was a boy scout. I would like to have a couple dollars when I came out of recovery, I can't imagine what it will be like. Running on full power. After everything I have done, all across western Canada, half a dozen small businesses, the drugs, the alcohol, the stress I have put my heart under and to find out that I only had about half the energy I was supposed to have, it is kind of a shocker.

On the final note, it is New Year's next week. Saw the heart doctor today; odds are I am perfectly fine. Looking like I don't need that pace maker, funny, misdiagnosed again. However, my father was diagnosed with schizophrenia and I know it is hereditary. And smoking pot actually does more harm than good for this disease. Again funny, one thing leaves and another appears. That's life, must move on and learn the lesson or how do you better yourself?

It is probably my diet and sleeping habits that affects my lack of energy and feelings of lifelessness. Everyone gets to the point when they feel it is time for a major change. Most know it is the right thing to do; few have the conviction to follow through. And fewer succeed in changing. I will do it, can you?